CLARION
Call of Love

Essays in Gratitude to
Archbishop
Lazar Puhalo

Clarion Call of Love:
Essays in Gratitude to Archbishop Lazar Puhalo
by the authors of Clarion Journal
of Spirituality and Justice
Copyright © 2018 St Macrina's Press

Cataloging-in-Publication Data

Puhalo, Lazar, 1938- ;Jersak, Brad, 1964- ;Dart, Ron, 1950-
Clarion Call of Love: Essays in Appreciation of Archbishop Lazar
Puhalo / eds. Brad Jersak, Ron S. Dart.
1. Puhalo, Lazar, 1938- . 2. Puhalo, Lazar, Festschrift.

ISBN-13: 978-1987710465
ISBN-10: 1987710460

Printed in the USA

Published by St Macrina's Press
Abbotsford, BC Canada
bradjersak@gmail.com

CLARION
Call of Love

Essays in Gratitude to
Archbishop
Lazar Puhalo

by authors of
Clarion Journal
of Spirituality and Justice

St Macrina's Press

ἡ ἐπιστολὴ ἡμῶν ὑμεῖς ἐστε, ἐγγεγραμμένη ἐν ταῖς καρδίαις ἡμῶν, γινωσκομένη καὶ ἀναγινωσκομένη ὑπὸ πάντων ἀνθρώπων, φανερούμενοι ὅτι ἐστὲ ἐπιστολὴ Χριστοῦ διακονηθεῖσα ὑφ᾽ ἡμῶν, ἐγγεγραμμένη οὐ μέλανι ἀλλὰ πνεύματι θεοῦ ζῶντος, οὐκ ἐν πλαξὶν λιθίναις ἀλλ᾽ ἐν πλαξὶν καρδίαις σαρκίναις.

You yourselves are our letter, written on our hearts, known and read by everyone, revealing that you are a letter of Christ, delivered by us, written not with ink but by the Spirit of the living God, not on stone tablets but on tablets of human hearts.

2 Cor. 3:2-3

Contents

Preface

Fifteen years ago, Archbishop Lazar Puhalo fired up the printing press of the All Saints of North America Monastery in Dewdney, BC and the *Clarion Journal of Spirituality and Justice* was born. He personally printed, folded, stapled and trimmed thousands of copies while imparting his wisdom to those of us who assisted him. After giving us three years of traction by running hardcopies, Vladika released the magazine for its launch into cyberspace. Since then, the journal has posted 1,950 articles (half of those by the six authors of this book, over 200 book reviews, had 870,000 page-views and won a national blog award. Not only that, but Abp. Lazar personally contributed 101 posts of his own, ranging from soaring patristic theology to clear-minded political commentary and heartfelt poetry!

After Abp. Lazar recently suffered a series of major health crises, Ron Dart suggested a number of the original co-editors and key authors compile a *festschrift* in his honour. In gratitude for Vladika's commitment to *Clarion,* to Christ-centered spirituality and public justice, and to our lives as individuals, each contributor has offered an essay reflecting a theme that we associate with Abp. Lazar's wisdom, expertise and interests. These articles cannot express the debt we owe him, but we're glad they reminded us it is a debt of love.

God grant you many years, Vladika
Pascha 2018
Reader Irenaeus

1

The First and Last Words of a Pastoral Prophet

Brad (Irenaeus) Jersak

First Words

I remember Archbishop Lazar's first words to me when we started engaging in 2003. Not *literally* his first words, but those that surely launched my journey toward Orthodoxy.

I had grown up in a good Baptist home, after which attended and graduated from a conservative Evangelical theological college. After marrying Eden, I was invited to ministry in her home church—Bethel Mennonite in Aldergrove, BC—where I was ordained and served with youth, young adults and outreach for a decade. In 1998, we joined another couple in planting a small-c charismatic church with a focus on serving those on the margins (people with disabilities, addicts, the poor).

Our time with the Mennonites and our church planting experience trained our hearts to long for Christ-centered justice in this world. Hoping to establish a magazine featuring the connection between spirituality and justice, I was introduced to my mentor, Ron Dart. He suggested we team up with Abp. Lazar at the All Saints of North America monastery in Dewdney, BC because Vladika was committed to these themes and willing to partner with us through the use of his monastery print shop.

And so I was introduced to this Gandalf-like character, complete with floor-length cassock, trailing white beard and sincere, piercing eyes. Collating magazines side-by-side with Vladika for countless hours afforded me the privilege of extensive conversations, and we began to discuss the faith-shift I was experiencing. The Anabaptists had already introduced me to nonviolent alternatives to penal substitutionary atonement theory. And in an experience that I regard in retrospect as a mystical intervention, these words pierced my heart:

"Stop telling people I was punishing my Son. That is not what was happening."

Of course, one does not exchange theologies based on attributing any passing phrase to God. But understand, my MA thesis was a 180-page apologetic for PSA titled "The Nature of Christ's Suffering and Substitution." I wrote, preached and evangelized a 5-point Calvinist PSA gospel, so the epiphany was my Damascus Road. I scurried back to the Bible, disciplining myself to re-examine the Scriptures I had previously used as the bulwark of my soteriology, assuming they described Christ's death as wrath-appeasement and divine abandonment. As a young fundamentalist, I had never regarded penal substitution as a theory of the atonement. It was the gospel—the *only* gospel, plain and simple. Alternatives were deemed liberal heresies. But with new eyes and more attentive ears, I waded back into the Scriptures and weighed alternative interpretations (ancient and modern) and as I did, the Jericho of my old atonement theology began crumbling around me.

There it was in Isaiah 53: "Yet *we ourselves* esteemed Him stricken, smitten of God, and afflicted. But He was pierced through for our transgressions, He was crushed for our iniquities." *WE* considered him stricken by God… Implication: he wasn't.

And again in Psalm 22: After reading the cry of dereliction in verse 1, we continue to verses 22-24. "For He has not despised nor abhorred the affliction of the afflicted; nor has He hidden His face from him; but when he cried to Him for help, He heard." While Christ existentially bore our despair, ontologically, not once does the Father turn his face away.

One can see how I was providentially ripened for catechism at the feet of Abp. Lazar. Today we might call this journey a "deconstruction," but Brian Zahnd as encouraged me towards the less violent language of art "reconstruction."

When layers of grime overshadow a masterpiece, one does not go to work with the iconoclasts knife. Time and care must be taken to strip away defilement without spoiling what is precious beneath.

In any case, in the fullness of my transition, I first encountered Abp. Lazar. One day, while working in the print shop with him, I tried to explain the difficulties of my previous worldview and my quest for a vision of the Cross more faithful to the truth of the gospel.

Vladika put it to me straightforwardly: "Are you

telling me you believed God cannot freely forgive sin but must first appease his wrath through the violent sacrifice of his firstborn son on the cross?" I responded that although his characterization might seem crass at first, it seemed to say exactly what I had been taught, believed and preached. Though more nuanced of PSA spins have emerged since the publication of *Stricken by God?* (and in part because of it), what he described was and remains the unvarnished and dominant Evangelical gospel. But for me, the sandy shores of my Calvinist premises were already being washed away. Now came the coup de grâce (lit., 'blow of mercy' or 'stroke of grace').

Archbishop Lazar replied, "I see your problem. You worship Molech—not Yahweh. Not Yahweh." Molech was the Canaanite god who demanded his wrath to be appeased by the fiery sacrifice of their firstborn children (Isa. 57:5, Jer. 194-:5, etc). "Something," Yahweh says, "that he had never spoken, commanded or even entered his mind." Archbishop Lazar is rather harsh assessment did not offend me. Rather, his words washed through me like the cold flood, awakening me. Something like scales fell off my spiritual eyes. My witness was no namby-pamby liberal—this was a hierarch stewarding the Patristic faith that gave us the deity of Christ, the dogma of Trinity and the Nicene Creed.

"You mean in Orthodoxy, you aren't *required* to believe in penal substitution?" I asked, hopeful.

"No, I mean in Orthodoxy, you are not *permitted* to believe in it," he replied firmly, adding, "And there are 350 million of us who have *never* believed it. We regard it as heresy."

That moment confirmed decisively the content (if not the Source) of my inner voice and renewed biblical studies. It marked the beginning of a series of falling dominoes that comprised my 10-year-long catechism at Vladika's feet. Once penal substitution fell, doctrines related to retribution began to topple in turn. If God truly is *love* in his essential nature (though Calvinists deny this), the *necessity* of eternal conscious torment, direct acts of divine genocide and literalist interpretations of wrath fall too.

What surprised me about this development was that I did not fall off the outer limbs of the Evangelical tree. Instead, Abp. Lazar drew me deep into the roots of historic Christianity as taught by the great early mothers and fathers of our faith.

Another of our Clarion conversations was so pivotal that I memorized Vladika's response verbatim. I was still struggling with the problem of Old Testament commands sanctioning violence. I could no longer live with "the Bible says it, I believe it, that settles it" when it came to Scriptures in which the narrator declares that God initiates calls to merciless slaughters, enslavement of women and children and even accommodating rape of enemy captives. Yes, that's in there. I read it and so do the "new atheists" who mock Christianity. Those among my Evangelical friends who could still hold an ideology of inerrancy could do so by either staying unaware of these texts or reading them in a cartoonish manner that allowed them to praise the Lord without empathy for real human victims. I was done with that.

When I queried Vladika about this, he insisted that the Old Testament is often a revelation primarily about us and our idolatrous images of God, awaiting the faithful picture that God in Christ would reveal through the Incarnation. One day I brought his attention to 1 Samuel 15. I was incredibly frustrated with the platitudes of those who affirmed that God commanded Samuel to command Saul to destroy every last Amalekite—man, woman, infant and domestic beast—especially when the narrator says that God's justification was the sins of their ancestors many centuries before.

I decided to put on my Evangelical hat to interrogate Archbishop Lazar on this troubling passage. That is, I assumed a posture towards the text that treated every word is God's inerrant truth, though I had come to see inerrancy as rather modernist. I read 1 Sam. 15 to Archbishop Lazar and asked him how it could be that the Abba whom Jesus Christ revealed as perfect love and relentless mercy could possibly issue such a command.

Without hesitation, he replied, "He didn't."

I countered, "But the Bible says He did."

He parried with these surprising words: "No, these are the words of Samuel, a cantankerous old bigot who would not let go of his prejudice, projecting his own malice, unforgiveness and need for vengeance into the mouth of Yahweh."

I was not to be deterred easily. I answered back, "But

it's not just Samuel saying it. The narrator says Yahweh spoke these words to Samuel."

"He didn't!"

"But Vladika, this is the Word of God."

That did it. At this point, Archbishop Lazar's face grew stern. His long index finger grew towards my face, correcting me with these firm words:

"NO! Jesus is the Word of God. And any scripture that claims to be a revelation of that God must bow to the living God when he came in the flesh. 'No man has seen God at any time, but God the only Son, who was in the bosom of the Father—He has made him known.'"

I was both duly chastened and filled with joy. The hair on my head stood up and my entire body tingled with goose flesh. I have never and will never forgot that lesson. It not merely a word about reading Samuel 15 or every Old Testament call to genocide. What Vladika made crystal clear is the truth that every conception of God has always been imperfect prior to the Incarnation of Jesus Christ as the final and only perfect revelation of God, fulfilling, completing and correcting all previous revelations.

It is on this premise that Christian orthodoxy is founded. It was on this premise that I wrote my book, A More Christlike God, dedicated to Vladika. In that book, I say very little beyond what Vladika has taught me since that day. Specifically, that if there is a God (forever a faith statement), that God is love. And God is love only, for every other attribute of God must every only be a facet of that one pure diamond. And if we want to know exactly what that love consists of, we look to the Incarnation. "If you've seen me," said Christ, "you have seen the Father." The apostle Paul declares to the Colossians that "Christ is the image of the invisible God" and "In him all the fullness of the Godhead dwelled in bodily form." Hebrews 1 adds that Christ alone "the radiance of God's glory and the exact representation of God's likeness."

Most importantly, this revelation of love comes to its clearest focus on the Cross, where we see Jesus Christ revealed God as self-giving, radically forgiving, co-suffering love. "He is a good and man-befriending God," says our liturgy. Or as Vladika's old friend, his eminence Archbishop Irénée (of the Archdiocese of Canada) says, "God is mercy only." Not "mercy plus…" Not "love, but also…" There is no literal divine anger, judgment or wrath apart from God's love. Such attributes, according to Hebrews 12, can ever only anthropomorphisms limited to expressions of Fatherly love. That is, what we call "God's wrath" is nothing other than the self-induced consequences or intrinsic judgement of our own turning from perfect love, though these may become the very venue for God's redemptive acts.

Vladika puts it this way, "The fire of the glory of the love of God extends to all, and our orientation to the fire of love determines whether we experience it as heaven or hell, but we hold to the great hope that it is a cleansing fire able to purge even the darkest of hearts."

These are the reflections I carry when I think of the Abp. Lazar's "first words" (to me).

Pastoral Prophet

I must add a word about Vladika's pastoral prophetic role. The Orthodox Church today, like ancient Judaism and Patristic Christianity, features a heavy imbalance of priests over prophets. The prophets of old, from Isaiah to Maximos, were discarded ignobly and sentenced to death by hierarchs prior to their posthumous canonization as saints. Further, it is an error of the West to regard prophet as raging contrarians when in fact their great motivation has always been primarily pastoral concern for sheep. When their words were biting, it was because they spoke on behalf of those on the margins who were downtrodden by economic, political and most of all, religious power structures.

Likewise, if Archbishop Lazar has been widely regarded as controversial, his prophetic edge can only be understood rightly in the context of pastoral care. He is frequently slandered and formally censured for speaking up on two fronts: his compassionate advocacy for LGBTQ young people and his rejection of the toll-house myth. Whether one agrees with his positions on these topics or not, I would plead for a clear-minded focus on his motives.

What drew Archbishop Lazar into these controversies was the pastoral impulse. He cares deeply for simple people who interpret the toll-houses literally and thus, live in terror of death and under the control of those who employ fear as a pastoral strategy. For Vladika, the issue is not about eschatological hairsplitting, but about the spiritual abuse of vulnerable parishioners.

Second, he waded into the question of homosexuality and transgenderism, not because he is a flaming liberal who disregards the teaching of the church around sexual sin, but because of the wave of suicides among young believers whose priests condemned even their orientation as an abomination beyond repentance and who were therefore doomed to hell. He saw the grave injustice and hypocrisy in this and made the mistake of naming it. On judgment day when he meets Christ, I suspect it is a mistake he will be relieved to have made. By refusing to play the game, Vladika has chosen to sacrifice influence rather than his soul. To my mind, he may never be a saint, but there's no question that he's faithfully fulfilled the role of pastoral prophet.

Whatever errors he is considered to have made in speaking for these groups, we ought never mistake the fact that he is practicing co-suffering love for the most fearful and the most rejected among us. If that motive is in question, one might ask after the motives of his opponents. In seeking to be faithful, the means need to be consistent with the ends. Even these controversial topics fall within the purview of the gospel Vladika preaches, distilled perfect in Christ's parable of the prodigal son. I see in Vladika a reflection of the who runs to the wayward son "even while a long way off."

"Last" Words

My essay title also referred to Vladika's last words. Again, not *literally* his last words, because he is still fully alive and may God grant him many years.

I refer to his last words because on two occasions, I believe both he and I were conscious of the real possibility he might be sharing his final words with me in this side of the veil. Within hours of his first stroke, I sat in ER beside his bed with my journal ready, ears open and recorder on. He called me close and shared through halting speech (but fully lucid mind) his distillation of the meaning of life and what is most important. Through his tears and my own, he spoke what was most precious by way of a patriarchal blessing. I rejoice to say that those 'last words' were entirely consistent with the life message he has been stewarding all along. In other words, what mattered most to Vladika in what might have been his final hour are the very truths we have heard long-term in all his homilies. Rather than sullying his words with my own paraphrase, I offer them verbatim as a gift to the reader in the final chapter of this work, titled "Sailing into the Winter Sun" after the title of his final journal.

2

The Political Theology of Archbishop Lazar Puhalo: High Tory

Ron S. Dart

Political Context

I initially met Archbishop Puhalo in the autumn of 1998. I was invited to the Canadian Orthodox Monastery in Dewdney British Columbia to discuss, at one level, the political situation in Canada. The reign of the Progressive Conservatives, undermined in many ways by Prime Minister Brian Mulroney (1984-1993), given his fondness for President Ronald Reagan, tended to equate conservatism in Canada with republicanism in the USA, had come to an end. Needless to say, many are the Orthodox in the USA that nod and genuflect uncritically to such republicanism and this deeply worried Archbishop Lazar.

The equally important dilemma in Canadian political life in the 1990s was that the emergence and growth of Preston Manning's Reform-Alliance Party (further right than the Progressive Conservatives) was dividing the centre and centre-right in Canada. It was such a contested clash within the interpretation of conservatives between an older High Toryism and Blue Conservatism that brought the Liberal Party to power for more than a decade

(Jean Chretien: 1993-2003 and Paul Martin: 2003-2006).

Such a redefinition of conservatism had been artic-
ulated and anticipated by Preston Manning's father,
Ernest Manning, in his 1967 political booklet and man-
ifesto of sorts, *Political Realignment: A Challenge to
Thoughtful Canadians* (for which the younger Preston
Manning did much of the research).

It was, therefore, this fragmenting and reductionistic
definition within Canadian political and public life about
the meaning and significance of a distinct Canadian
High Toryism (being clear cut by American republican
conservatism) that brought Archbishop Lazar and I
together in the autumn of 1998. There was, in the 1990s,
an attempt to reclaim the older meaning of High Toryism
contra Blue Conservatism by David Orchard, and his
book, *The Fight for Canada: Four Centuries of Resistance to American Expansionism* (1993) was a portal
for many into recovering a more classical notion of
Canadian economic nationalism contra the free trade-
FTA-NAFTA internationalism of the decade.

David Orchard, Archbishop Lazar and I did a variety
of events together both at the Monastery and University
of the Fraser Valley (where I teach in the Political Science Department). My ongoing lectures at UFV (and
some published material in newspapers and alternate
magazines) on Canadian nationalism attracted Archbishop Lazar to my efforts. We had a lively introductory
conversation and it became most obvious we were on
the same political page. At the same time, I was also in
the process of starting a political magazine, shaped by

S.T. Coleridge's short lived *The Friend.* I called my magazine *The Friend: Ancient Roots, New Routes.* Archbishop Lazar was keen to see the magazine launched well and was most supportive of the effort and publication of it (contributing articles himself). Given the fact that Synaxis Press was nested at the Monastery, he suggested that he would be quite willing to publish my booklets and books on Red/High Toryism.

Synaxis Press and Red/High Toryism

I was somewhat disappointed with the 2004 publication of Andrew Sopko's introductory book, *The Culture of Co-Suffering Love: The Theology of Archbishop Lazar Puhalo.* Sopko had erred, as do many who define and understand theology in a limited manner, by ignoring Archbishop Lazar's political theology. I can understand Sopko's literary gaff of sorts—he neither understood the Canadian historic or political tradition and ethos. Hence it was easier for him to simply omit this essential read of Archbishop Lazar's more comprehensive and grounded notion of theology. But to censor out Archbishop Lazar's political theology is to seriously distort how Archbishop Lazar understands the integrative nature of theology and sanitize his thinking and public commitments.

The task, though, when doing political philosophy and engaging in historic political life is to discern and clarify which form of political theory-activism can best embody—in thought, word and deed—the good life or the commonwealth (commonweal).

The fact that Andrew Sopko (being American) knew little about the unique Anglo-Canadian High-Red Tory way meant that he was somewhat hindered and hobbled in his approach to include in his book a chapter on Archbishop Lazar's Red/High Tory political theology. Such a synthesis within the North American context is rare and practically absent within Orthodoxy in North America. When they actually *do* political theology, virtually no North American Orthodox theologians ponder, internalize, articulate and act on the unique Canadian Red/High Tory tradition and heritage. Through our meeting, Archbishop Lazar and I (a High Tory catholic Anglican) were able to thread together a dialogue between political Orthodoxy and High Tory Anglicanism, and the role of Synaxis Press was to incarnate such a meeting of a vision.

The fact that by the 1990s, political life in Canada had doffed the leadership cap of the Liberal Party (with its economic attraction to the USA) and the equally disturbing fact that Manning-led Blue Conservatives were clearcutting historic Canadian High Toryism. This meant a variety of tasks had to be engaged: overcoming the serious problem of cultural and intellectual amnesia that dogged many, retelling the classical tale and participating in the formal political process at a variety of significant levels.

The fact that Synaxis Press was a vibrant publishing reality meant that Archbishop Lazar was front and centre in getting the classical tale out. He intuitively sensed that we in Canada hold a deeper and older vision of what constitutes the common good and the shaping of meaningful citizenship, but he was weak on the historic details. This is why he walked the extra mile to publish a variety of my works on High-Red Toryism and contributed to many a conference at the monastery on the topic, education being a necessary aspect of rebuilding the ancient city.

The publication in the autumn of 1998 by Synaxis Press of my booklet, *The Red Tory Vision: Retrieving the Conservative Tradition,* was the first in a series of educational attempts to recover what had been, for the most part, forgotten within the Canadian political and public sphere (or, worse yet, co-opted for right of centre purposes). The initial booklet was followed in 1999 by the larger book, *The Red Tory Tradition: Ancient Roots, New Routes."* In an autographed copy of his *The Fight for Canada,* David Orchard had this to say about my writing on Toryism: "Looking forward to working with you to publish the intellectual foundations of a New Red Toryism."

Archbishop Lazar, David Orchard (and his committed and energetic team) and I (along with many others) were working from many angles to counter the right of centre drift in Canada with an alternate vision. We had become, in many ways, the ginger group and fifth column.

Searching for Canada: The Red Tory Journey was published in 2000—more fine authors were brought into the fray: Clarence Bolt, Norman Knowles, Anthony Hall/Splitting the Sky, David Baswick, Robin Mathews, Archbishop Lazar and myself. The tale was being filled out in yet a fuller manner. The emerging momentum and interest inspired Archbishop Lazar to publish in 2001 my book of political poetry, *Crosshairs: Being Poetic, Being Political, Being Canadian* and the birthing of a distinctive Red Tory Journal: *The Red Tory Journal: The Spirit of the Canadian Ethos*. Many of the significant and historic Canadian intellectuals were included in the magazine: Dalton Camp, Stephen Leacock, George Grant, Joe Clark, Mazo de la Roche and others.

The home of thought that had once built this country and that had been razed by a notion of Hegelian progressive liberalism was being rebuilt brick by brick, stone by stone. There were some interesting and strange bedfellows in the rebuilding but Archbishop Lazar was quite willing to include them in both the publications through Synaxis Press and conferences we organized together. Needless to say, this did not endear him to many Orthodox who were decidedly right of centre in their religious and political leanings.

I should note at this point that the much-contested article by Gad Horowitz in the mid-1960s, "Conservatism, Liberalism, and Socialism in Canada: An Interpretation," made it intriguingly clear that Canadian Toryism had much in common with the political left rather than a form of conservatism that was decidedly on the political right. Horowitz drew from a variety of sources to illustrate his point, and George Grant factored large in such an interpretation. It was this read of Grant by Horowitz that illuminated how and why Canadian political thought and action parted paths with the USA and how Canadian conservatives of the Albertan Manning Reform-Alliance types had little in common with historic Anglo-Canadian High Toryism. Archbishop Lazar intuitively understood this left-of-centre Canadian High Tory nationalist tendency and he used Synaxis Press to further such a vision.

Robin Mathews (who knew the work of Horowitz well) is probably one of the finest Canadian political poets of the 20th century. He stands very much on the shoulders of Milton Acorn and Dorothy Livesay (two of our finest Canadian political poets). Archbishop Lazar and Robin Mathews befriended one another and Robin became essential to our work in recovering the High/Red Tory way. I suggested to Archbishop Lazar that I do a book on Mathews, and he eagerly supported such a publication through Synaxis Press. *Robin Mathews: Crown Prince of Canadian Political Poets* was published in 2002.

The larger tale had to be told, though, as the conservative clearcutting ever continued in a rapacious way and manner. The fact that in 2003 Peter MacKay worked with Stephen Harper to merge the Progressive Conservatives with the Canadian Alliance into the Conservative Party of Canada meant that High Toryism was becoming an endangered species. Again, Archbishop Lazar who suggested I write a larger book on the Canadian family tree of High Toryism. Voila: *The Canadian High Tory Tradition: Raids on the Unspeakable* was published in 2004. The struggle to defend classical High Toryism at the public and political level was waning—right-of-centre conservatism was waxing. But merely to retreat, to fold our hands in defeat, was not an option. Those who forget and forfeit the wisdom of the past live in time to regret such a reality—consequences often then become the teacher.

The victory of Stephen Harper in the 2006 Federal election meant that a form of Albertan conservatism (even further right than Manning and tribe) had taken front stage. The Calgary School of political philosophy were in their heyday. The older Tory tale needed to be more fully told.

Again, Archbishop Lazar via Synaxis Press suggested I do a book on Stephen Leacock (one of the best Canadian humourists and political thinkers) whose affinity with both Manning, Harper and the Calgary School would be null. *Stephen Leacock: Canada's Red Tory Prophet* was published in 2006 to provide an alternate notion of conservatism to Harper and tribe. Terry Glavin also did a lengthy interview with me for *Georgia Straight* in 2006, and the article was published as "Stephen Harper is No Tory" *(Georgia Straight*: Feb. 29, 2006).

There can be no doubt that Archbishop Lazar played a front-stage role as publisher (Synaxis Press) and event organizer in encouraging a sort of High-Red Tory resistance and opposition to the growth and dominance of the Americanization of Canadian conservatism through the vehicle of right-of-centre think-tanks and the Conservative Party of Canada. In short, Archbishop Lazar's notion of theology was deeply immersed in the larger political, economic, historic and social issues of the time—his High Tory political theology must be noted when understanding how he (and he was unusual in doing this) interpreted his Orthodoxy within the Canadian context. But, there was yet more to his thinking, activism and irenic approach.

Clarion Journal and Archbishop Lazar

The 1990s brought the emergence in the Fraser Valley of a growing number of former conservative evangelicals who were reaching towards the further shore for a greater vision of faith. Their quest birthed a magazine in the autumn of 2003. *Clarion: Journal of Justice and Spirituality* brought together creative minds and imaginations in legitimate discontent, searching for of a fuller vision beyond the confines of right-of-centre Evangelical politics and neo-Calvinist theology (which was in ascendance).

The narrow theology and politics that pandered to the political right was not the path the more probing thinkers of *Clarion* wished to go. It is one thing, though, to be taken by the idea of publishing a regular journal on timely topics. It is quite another to actually publish hardcopies of such a magazine. Yet again, Archbishop Lazar stepped into the breach. He graciously offered to print the initial copies of *Clarion* from his press at the monastery. Many were the hours we spent at the monastery, rolling out coloured copies, then collating, stapling and trimming had to be done. The larger vision of *Clarion* was to reflect on the legitimate need to integrate, in thought, word and deed, the interest in spirituality (quite trendy in many ways) with political justice (locally and globally).

The hardcopy publishing of *Clarion* from 2003-2006 was done, again and again, by Archbishop Lazar from the printing press at the monastery. Such a generous reality brought together many with little or no background within the time-tried Orthodox way to their first encounter with Orthodoxy. Evangelicals meet Orthodox. This journey certainly has many a precedent, the most significant being the substantive conversion of many Campus Crusade devotees to Antiochene Christianity.

Archbishop Lazar not only printed all of the 2003-2006 editions of *Clarion* at the monastery but he also wrote many a missive for the ever-expanding magazine. Many articles in *Clarion* that later became chapters in his prolific book output. He is probably the most published Orthodox theologian in North America, but by daring to challenge, at times, the Orthodox hierarchy, he has been kept from the centre of the Orthodox Church of America's publishing hub, seminary life and lecture circuit. I suppose, in many ways, Archbishop Lazar has been a prophet of sorts to the Orthodox community in North America and as such, he has been held in much suspicion by the ruling Sanhedrin. But, such a marginalization has, in an indirect way, meant a certain irenic tone has brought him into contact with questioning and questing Evangelicals.

Clarion was published in hardback from 2003-2006

and from 2006 to the present, has been posted on a website. Archbishop Lazar has continued to post articles on the website. Now, with the launch of Canadian Orthodox Broadcasting System more than decade ago (from the monastery), many of his interviews have not only dealt with the political but also historic themes that relate to current events.

Canadian Orthodox Broadcasting System

Synaxis Press has published the wide range of Archbishop Lazar's writings, including books on political theology. *Clarion* (paper magazine
and website) has also included many of Archbishop Lazar's articles. But the Canadian Orthodox Broadcasting System has made the appearances of Archbishop Lazar in homilies, liturgy and dialogue sessions even more personal and available to a broader audience.

Archbishop Lazar and I did many a dialogue event on the Canadian Orthodox Broadcasting System, embracing a wide-ranging compendium of topics such as Red Toryism, Canadian Nationalism, Canadian Literature and Culture, Zionism and the Palestinians, Anglo-Orthodox dialogue, reflections with Brad Jersak and Kevin Miller on the film *Hellbound?*, Tradition, traditions and traditionalism, Desert Fathers/Mothers, *Philokalia*, Ephraim of Syria, Western and Eastern Christianity, Erasmus, the layered nature of the North American evangelical ethos, culture wars, science and theology and much else. There were few subjects that were not covered in our many live discussions (the train in the background ever amusing attentive listeners). The Anglican/Orthodox dialogues also contributed to our launch of the Canadian Fellowship of St. Alban and St. Serge in 2012.

The sample list of topics Archbishop Lazar and I covered (with many others) indicate his broad range of interests. He is in many ways an Orthodox Humanist, just as High Tories are humanists in the classical sense. That is, those with curious minds who are interested in every aspect of the human condition.

The 2010 theatrical release of Kevin Miller's controversial documentary, *Hellbound?* featured on-screen appearances by Archbishop Lazar. The Orthodox position on hell is much more nuanced and layered than the standard vision that Reformed and Evangelical traditions often strenuously hold high and defend. Kevin's recently edited book, *Hellrazed?* (2017) includes an article by Archbishop Lazar ("The True Gift of Hellbound?") that succinctly summarizes both Kevin's important work and an Orthodox response to literalist notions of hell. Indeed, Archbishop Lazar has dared to question aspects of Orthodox fundamentalism and challenged Evangelicals to enlarge their vision of the *eschaton*.

I would also like to mention, by way of conclusion, the respect Archbishop Lazar has for Thomas Merton. Archbishop kindly printed a variety of publications on Merton for the Thomas Merton Society of Canada (TMSC). His own booklet, *Thomas Merton and the Hesychastic Tradition: The Problem of Inner Human*

Suffering is worth reading many times over. The fact that Archbishop Lazar had a more nuanced read of Merton put him at odds, yet again, with his decades-long nemesis (Seraphim Rose), whom he had challenged on the controversial "toll-house" issue. The fact that Archbishop Lazar could have such a positive attitude towards Thomas Merton contra Seraphim Rose is but another pointer to his more engaging form of Orthodoxy.

Conclusion

I mentioned at the outset that as much as I appreciated Andrew Sopko's *For a Culture of Co-Suffering Love: The Theology of Archbishop Lazar Puhalo,* I was somewhat disappointed by his failure to include in his book the political theology (Orthodox High Toryism) of Archbishop Lazar. I have, hopefully, corrected such an omission. I have also mentioned the way Archbishop Lazar has been a prophetic gadfly of sorts to certain forms of ethnic and fundamentalist Orthodoxy and those brands of Orthodoxy that lean to the political right.

Abp. Lazar has also been an inviting voice to many raised within a conservative Evangelical ethos that tends towards the political right and Calvinist theology. His ongoing dialogue with a variety of Evangelicals is of a different order than that which often occurs between the Orthodox and Evangelicals (which tend to be a reactive form of conservatism). His understanding of Orthodoxy has a different scent and flavour to what we saw in the Campus Crusaders turn to Orthodoxy in the 1980s.

Appendix: Miscellaneous Reflections

I have often asked Archbishop Lazar about a variety of topics he had either spoken or written about that deserved more commentary—a few final thoughts.

1. Archbishop Lazar wrote a finely-tuned paper on Florovsky and Bulgakov, tipping his hat much more to Florovsky. He mentioned to me if he wrote the essay again, he would have been more generous to Bulgakov.

2. We often chatted about Father Alexander Schmemann and John Meyendorff—he had the highest regard for the former but held serious doubts about the historic depth of the latter. This made for many an interesting conversation, given the fact I had corresponded with Meyendorff when he was alive.

3. Archbishop Lazar often told me he thought one of his better books was *Culture, Commonweal and Personhood*. He mentioned to me that he thought his chapter, "The Limits of Ecumenical Dialogue" was, in some ways, too harsh—he would have been more gracious and elastic if he wrote the chapter again.

4. The three books Archbishop thought were his best were *Culture, Commonweal and Personhood; Not By Bread Alone: Homilies on the Gospel According to St. Matthew* and *Freedom to Believe: Personhood and Freedom in Orthodox Christian Ontology*.

5. It is significant that Archbishop Lazar published my small booklet *Roderick High-Brown: Canada's Green Prophet*. Archbishop Lazar's final public event

(followed by his serious strokes a few days later) was at a two-day conference titled "A Sacramental Approach to Ecology" (October 6-7, 2017). The monastery played a significant role in coordinating this two-day conference with Trinity Western University. It was held in honour of the Ecumenical Patriarch Bartholomew (with his blessing). Indeed, it was fully ecumenical—signifying a journey travelled by Archbishop Lazar from a position in which the West was often vilified—the vision has become more nuanced and refined over the decades.

6. Archbishop Lazar was related to Mikhail Kournossoff and Mikhail's two-volume autobiography, *In the Crucible of Revolution: A Personal account of life in Tsarist Russia, the Russian Revolution…and beyond* and *From Purgatory to Paradise: A refugee from Stalinism discovers the joy and hardships of life in Canada as he journeys from an opulent life in Imperial Russia to a remarkable life as a Canadian farmer.*

These volumes were edited and published by Archbishop Lazar and Bishop Varlaam. Needless to say, the Russian Orthodox connection is near and dear to both Abp. Lazar and Bp. Varlaam—and Mikhail Kournossoff's decidedly left-of-centre thinking and life in the Fraser Valley had an impact on Abp. Lazar's High Tory politics.

7. George Ignatieff (1913-1989), like Mikhail Kournossoff, was an exile from Russia after the Revolution in 1917. Ignatieff, unlike Kournossoff, became a prominent civil servant at the highest levels of Canadian political life. Ignatieff was the Canadian ambassador to

Yugoslavia from 1956-1958 when Tito (1892-1980) was in power. Archbishop Lazar had some affinity with George Ignatieff's Russian roots, his Orthodoxy and Ignatieff's peacemaking commitments through the Pearson administration. Archbishop Lazar once told me that Tito asked Ignatieff "how he, being an educated, cultured and thoughtful man could possibly take religion with any seriousness." Ignatieff replied, "I take religion seriously because I am educated, cultured and thoughtful"—to which Tito moved onto other topics.

8. Archbishop Lazar was good friends with Marguerite Ritchie (1919-2016). Marguerite was at the forefront of women's rights in Canada. She was the first woman in Canada (as a lawyer) to be admitted to Queen's Counsel (in 1963) and founder of the Canadian Human Rights Institute in 1974. There are some lovely photos of Archbishop Lazar and Marguerite Ritchie together at the monastery.

9. Harry Rankin (1920-2002) was one of the longest sitting left-of-centre members of the Vancouver City Council. The friendship between Rankin and Abp. Lazar goes both to 1963 when both men were working on behalf of Vancouverites who lived in deplorable housing conditions. Their friendship continued until Rankin's death in 2002. Archbishop Lazar mentioned to me that he visited Harry Rankin shortly before his death and Rankin had said, "You social democrats have a lot to answer for." Archbishop Lazar and I have also had many a fine chat about Judy LaMarsh and Paul Hellyer.

10. I have mentioned some of the names above to clarify the fact that Archbishop Lazar had definite public and political leanings that included Mikhail Kournossoff, George Ignatieff, Marguerite Ritchie, Harry Rankin (and his wife Connie Fogel) and David Orchard. Archbishop Lazar never tired of mentioning his fondness for our rogue High Tory Prime Minister, John Diefenbaker and George Grant's moderate defence of him in *Lament for a Nation*.

11. I think it can be fairly suggested that Archbishop Lazar's political and public thinking was a blend of classical Anglo-Canadian High Toryism and a thoughtful yet moderate embrace of soft left liberalism—needless to say, there are some affinities between such notions of the common good.

3

Restorative Justice:[1]
Then, Now and a Dream

Wayne Northey

In Appreciation

This is dedicated to an amazing man of faith, Archbishop Lazar Puhalo. His stalwart leadership in scholarship interacting with many wider cultural issues; in exercising a consistent and persistent prophetic voice in response to a wide array of justice and peace issues; in mentoring and encouraging all kinds of the faithful within and outside the Orthodox Tradition; in offering hospitality to a great number of pilgrims over the years – to name only a few examples – has contributed significantly to the Church in the province of British Columbia where he resided and ministered, but across the world as well.

With deep respect and appreciation,
Wayne Northey

Restorative Justice Then

In 1974 two youths who had been drinking and had been "talked to" by the police already, took out their frustrations on the small community of Elmira, Ontario,

Canada by doing damage to twenty-two different vehicles and homes. Several months later the youths pleaded guilty to the charges, and the Judge ordered a Pre-Sentence Report. The Mennonite Probation Officer writing up the report discussed the case with the local Mennonite court volunteer. As it turned out, both had been reading recent publications by the "Law Reform Commission of Canada" in which it had been stated *that reconciliation played an important role in criminal justice.* They also knew that *reconciliation* was the central concept of their Christian faith, one committed to *peacemaking.* They decided to suggest a novel sentencing idea to the Judge: *ordering offenders first to "make it right" with their victims.*

The Judge indicated that the notion had lots of merit, but it was simply not done in Western jurisprudence. He made a fateful choice nonetheless when he decided "Why not?"; and put the sentencing over until the youths had met each of the victims who were willing. Out of that resultant positive experience arose the first ever "Victim Offender Reconciliation Project (VORP)," later to become known widely as Victim Offender Mediation.

This so-called "Elmira Case"[2] became a kind of proverbial shot that echoed around the world; acknowledged widely as the first ever justice system programmatic expression of Restorative Justice in the modern world.

By happenstance, providential for me at least, two years later I became second Director of that program, under Mennonite Central Committee Ontario. That launched me on a wonderful Restorative Justice journey ever since.

A Bit of History and Anthropology[3]

To set a context, some simplified historical and anthropological comments would be helpful.

History

Almost a millennium ago, in the late 11th century, European history underwent a *revolutionary* upheaval some in fact call "The Papal Revolution" (Berman, 1983/1997). During this time, the Church under Pope Gregory VII moved to consolidate its power over all souls and kings of Europe; the first great universities began to emerge; and the Western legal tradition started to take shape, as new laws based on newly discovered Roman Justinian law codes were formulated for study and eventual promulgation throughout the Western world.

In a fateful interplay between Church and Society, the secular realm began to follow the lead of how the Church dealt with its *religious heretics*. These "*social heretics*" began to emerge under new state law codes as "criminals" whose victims were no longer the actual victims, but eventually "*Rex*" or "*Regina*" in the British common law system instituted throughout Britain's history and Commonwealth, or "We the People" under the United States Constitution, etc.

The evolution of emerging criminal justice systems in the West turned away from *community restoration and victim centred justice* towards *state and offender centred justice*. The former had been a dominant approach in the ancient Hebrew culture; in Roman society when applied to its own citizens; and in most pre- and post-colonial worldwide indigenous cultures; in pre-11th century Europe as well.

As Norwegian criminologist Nils Christie wrote provocatively, the state began thereby to *steal the criminal conflict from the community.*[4] It is still a shock for some victims to discover that they are not even named on the court docket, having for instance a millennium ago been displaced by *Rex, Regina* or *"We the People"*. One victim of rape I know of describes a fantasy of phoning Queen Elizabeth in Buckingham Palace on each anniversary of the assault to ask her how she is doing!

The *purpose* of the law shifted dramatically as well. Earlier, the emphasis had been on *making the victim and violated community whole again*, what in the ancient Hebrew culture was called "restoring *shalom*". With the eventual rise however of monarchical power, and later with the emergence of nation states, the purpose became *to uphold the authority of the realm/state*. This only accelerated with the emergence of the modern "state" in Europe between about 1450 and 1650 (Cavanaugh, 2011, p.9).

There was dominant Western religious undergirding of this approach which led to a marriage of law and religion[5] that placed, on the one hand, *primary emphasis upon the offender's violation of the law* while dropping any concern for *rehabilitation of the victim and restoration of peace to the community*. On the other hand, it drew on *Roman slave law as model* for meting out the worst of punishments imaginable upon the offender.[6] This form of response to crime as we know is *retributive* or *punitive justice*, and has dominated Western jurisprudence for a millennium.

Ubiquitous Cultural Scapegoating Violence and Criminal Justice

Where did such violent notions of punishment originate?

When the above question is asked generically, even of all cultures, anthropologist René Girard argues that the *founding moment* of every society known to history is in fact *violence*. All human societies then initiate a *scapegoat mechanism* in order to contain the violence and restore social cohesion.

Such a *scapegoat mechanism* arises to siphon the violence away from the community, thereby creating peace for a time for the rest of society. In religious cultures, this kind of violence invariably took the form of myths, rituals, and prohibitions legitimizing the violence against the scapegoated target or targets. In Christian cultures, this form of violence for instance especially in response to offenders, was supported and spread by the *satisfaction theory* of the *atonement* (why Christ died)[7]. In the secular West, the ultimate instance of the same dynamic in sheer numbers is the Holocaust. One could adduce myriad further examples: destruction of indigenous peoples and cultures worldwide; enslavement and oppression of Blacks in America; the mass murder of Tutsis in Rwanda, etc., etc. Girard claims there is no culture or society free of this *foundational scapegoat mechanism.*

It was precisely over against the excesses of various forms of scapegoating violence that well-meaning Christian philanthropists tried in 1790, in Philadelphia, Pennsylvania, to move away from *physical punishments* towards an emphasis instead upon *reformation* of the criminal. If only they could lock wrongdoers into a jail cell with a Bible and a rule of silence, surely the violence would cease, and the criminal would become "*penitent*"! The new institution became of course known as a "*penitentiary*". The new *motive* was *rehabilitation*, not *retribution*. The first such "penitentiary" was the repurposed Walnut Street Jail in Philadelphia.

The idea caught on throughout the Western world like wildfire. But, it soon became evident that, whereas former means of scapegoating administered *physical* wounds that eventually would heal, the penitentiary began to inflict *psychic* harms that rarely ever mended. Though not the intent, a *new scapegoat mechanism* arose in the form of the penitentiary that indeed tended to destroy the very *soul* and *self-worth* of the prisoner. Then where did that lost soul ever after fit into society?[8]

Early in the development of Restorative Justice in Canada, Professor Vern Redekop[9] authored a widely received piece: *Scapegoats, the Bible, and Criminal*

Justice: Interacting with René Girard (1993). In it he posed the question:

> Is it possible that what *we* call a criminal justice system is really a scapegoat mechanism? (p. 1, emphasis in original).

He then analysed Girard's thesis on ubiquitous cultural scapegoat mechanisms; and answered the question he posed affirmatively (later receiving Girard's approbation). Redekop wrote:

> It [*is*] possible to think of the criminal justice system as *one gigantic scapegoat mechanism for society* (p. 33, emphasis in original).

He explained:

> When one considers how much crime is unreported, how few crimes are brought to trial and among those how few result in conviction and prison sentences it turns out that we in Canada imprison in the order of 3% of criminals… This tiny percentage of offenders who are severely punished can be thought of as *a collective scapegoat for society*. Those individual criminals who warrant sensational news coverage, can function as scapegoats themselves[10] (pp. 33 and 34, emphasis added).

In this context of criminal scapegoating, Restorative Justice poses perhaps the most troubling yet simple rhetorical question: *"Why harm people who harm people to teach people that harming people is wrong?"*

The Restorative Justice vision moves away from a warmaking, *"stigmatizing shaming"* scapegoat mechanism to a *"reintegrative shaming"*[11], peacemaking way of nonviolence in a bid to break definitively with the endless cycles of recurrent scapegoating violence in Western and Western-based criminal justice.

Restorative Justice Now

In less than half a century, Restorative Justice has become, if not a household name, one to reckon with in criminal justice virtually in any part of the Western world, and in countries under Western cultural influence – which is to say almost everywhere.

In Canada not only did *Restorative Justice* in 1975 find first criminal justice system expression anywhere in the West. There was subsequently the development of a related community justice expression, *Circle Sentencing,* another Canadian first that began in Canada's North, the Yukon Territories, in 1992, drawing on indigenous ways of doing justice[12]. Another Canadian first was in 1994 when the first Circle spontaneously happened around a released sex offender who by law was to be returned from prison to the community – in this case to Hamilton Ontario.[13] This development became known as *Circles of Support and Accountability (CoSA)*. Both later Restorative Justice programs have spread worldwide.

A fourth Canadian first was launched just in British Columbia by Catholic Charities Justice Services (June

4, 2016[14]): *Healing Circles of Support (HCS)* that forms a supportive Circle around a victim when other supports fall away. Time will tell how widely this initiative will be embraced.

Other Restorative Justice initiatives that have spread worldwide include:

- Victim Offender Mediation – based on the original Elmira Case in Canada;
- Family Group Conferencing/Family Group Decision Making;
- Conferencing (pre- and post-sentencing, pre-release)
- Restorative cautioning (Police);
- Restorative Practices in schools

As well, prison chaplaincy the world over has embraced Restorative Justice practices[15]; as do worldwide prison visitation programs; and a range of various community justice initiatives.

Restorative Justice: Future

In 2004 Desmond Tutu published a wonderful book: *God Has a Dream: a Vision of Hope For Our Time.* He drew on the language of arguably one of the most famous speeches of all in recent times by Dr. Martin Luther King, Jr.: "I Have a Dream," delivered August 28, 1963 at the Lincoln Memorial, Washington DC. Part of the speech went like this:

I have a dream that one day this nation will

rise up and live out the true meaning of its creed: "We hold these truths to be self-evident, that all men are created equal."

I have a dream that one day on the red hills of Georgia, the sons of former slaves and the sons of former slave owners will be able to sit down together at the table of brotherhood.

I have a dream that one day even the state of Mississippi, a state sweltering with the heat of injustice, sweltering with the heat of oppression, will be transformed into an oasis of freedom and justice.

I have a dream that my four little children will one day live in a nation where they will not be judged by the color of their skin but by the content of their character.

I have a *dream* today!

I have a dream that one day, down in Alabama, with its vicious racists, with its governor having his lips dripping with the words of "interposition" and "nullification" — one day right there in Alabama little black boys and black girls will be able to join hands with little white boys and white girls as sisters and brothers.

I have a *dream* today!

I have a dream that one day every valley shall be exalted, and every hill and mountain shall be made low, the rough places will be made plain, and the crooked places will be made straight; "and the glory of the Lord shall be revealed and all flesh shall see it together."

This is our hope, and this is the faith that I go back to the South with (King, Jr., 1963).

Amen!

Endnotes

1. A massive body of literature has emerged. A superb early study is Restoring Justice (Strong and Van Ness, 1997). A great early overview of the wider context is The Expanding Prison (Cayley, 1998). The first major study was Changing Lenses (Zehr, 1990) - considered a classic. The two best Christian theological studies are Chris Marshall's Beyond Retribution: A New Testament Vision for Justice, Crime, and Punishment (Eerdmans, Grand Rapids, 2001); and Compassionate Justice: An Interdisciplinary Dialogue with Two Gospel Parables on Law, Crime, and Restorative Justice (Eugene Oregon: Cascade Books, 2012.) An anthology of early writings on Restorative Justice is Restorative Justice: Ideas, Values, and Debates, Gerry Johnstone (Devon, UK: Willan Publishing, 2002). The first and enduring Restorative Justice website is at <http://restorativejustice.org/>

2. See a fuller account in Dean Peachey's "The Kitchener Experiment" (1989).

3. I am drawing on the work of Berman (1983/1997), Strong and Van Ness (1997), and Girard, in particular: (1977); (1986); (1987) and (2001).

4. Nils Christie wrote: "The victim in a criminal case is a sort of double loser in our society… He is excluded from

any participation in his own conflict. His conflict is stolen by the state, a theft which in particular is carried out by professionals (1981, p. 93)." He drew upon his earlier classic essay entitled "Conflicts as property" (1977).

5. See Gorringe (1996).

6. Herman Bianchi explicates this extensively in Justice as Sanctuary (1994).

7. See Gorringe (1996).

8. Michel Foucault's *Discipline and Punish: The Birth of the Modern Prison* (1978) presents this well.

9. Professor Redekop has been working creatively in conflict studies for decades. You may see more of his work, also in relation to René Girard, at <http://ustpaul.ca/index.php?mod=employee&id=48> (last accessed March 20, 2017).

10. Gil Bailie (1995) supplies a particularly sinister example, the 1989 execution of serial killer Theodore Bundy, when hundreds of men, women and children camped outside the Florida prison in a festive spirit one reporter likened to a Mardi Gras. The same reporter described the event as:

> … a brutal act… [done] in the name of civilization (p. 79).

Bailie reflects on that commentary thus:

> It would be difficult to think of a more succinct summation of the underlying anthropological dynamic at work: a brutal act done in the name of civilization, an expulsion or execution that results in social harmony. Clearly, after the shaky justifications based on deterrence or retribution have fallen away, this is the stubborn fact that remains: a brutal act is done in the name of civilization. If we humans become too morally troubled by the brutality to revel in the glories of the civilization made possible by it, we will simply have

to reinvent culture. This is what Nietzsche saw through a glass darkly. This is what Paul sensed when he declared the old order to be a dying one (I Cor. 7:31). This is the central anthropological issue of our age (ibid,p. 79, emphasis in original).

11. The classic book on this idea is Braithwaite (1989). A good brief online resource is found here: <https://learn.bu. edu/bbcswebdav/pid-1942479-dt-content-rid- 6162758_1/ courses/14sprgmetcj602_ol/week06/metcj602_W06L01T04 _Reintegrative.html> (last accessed March 25, 2017).

12. See Stuart (1997). See also Pranis, K., Stuart, B., & Wedge. M. (2003.)

13. That story is told at <http://cosacanada.com/history-of-cosa-canada> (last accessed March 25, 2017).

14. See: Healing Circles of Support here: <http://rcav.org/ prison-and-justice-services>.

15. An international journal reflecting this, sent to chaplains worldwide, is Justice Reflections at <http://www.justicereflections.org.uk>.

References

Bailie, Gil (1995). *Violence Unveiled: Humanity at the Crossroads*, New York: Crossroad.

Berman, Harold J. (1983/1997). *Law and Revolution: The Formation of the Western Legal Tradition*, Cambridge: Harvard University Press.

Bianchi, Herman (1994). *Justice as Sanctuary: Toward a New System of Crime Control*. Bloomington: Indiana University Press. (A recent republication is in 2009/10 by Oregon: Wipf & Stock.)

Braithwaite, John (1989). *Crime, Shame and Reintegration*,

New York: Cambridge University Press.

Cavanaugh, William T. (2011). *Migrations of the Holy: God, State, and the Political Meaning of the Church*, Grand Rapids: Eerdmans.

Cayley, David (1998). *The Expanding Prison: The Crisis in Crime and Punishment and the Search for Alternatives*, Toronto: Anansi Press.

Christie, Nils (1977). "Conflicts as Property", *British Journal of Criminology*, 17, 1 – 19.

Christie, Nils (1981). *Limits to Pain,* Oxford: Martin Robertson.

Foucault, Michel (1977). *Discipline and Punish: The Birth of the Modern Prison*, Hammondsworth: Penguin.

Girard, René (1977) *Violence and the Sacred.* Baltimore: Johns Hopkins University;

_____(1986) *The Scapegoat*, Baltimore: The Johns Hopkins University Press

_____(1987); *Things Hidden since the Foundation of the World: Research Undertaken in Collaboration with Jean-Michel Oughourlian and Guy Lefort,* Stanford: Stanford University Press.

_____ (2001) *I See Satan Fall Like Lightning*, New York: Orbis.

Gorringe, Timothy (1996). *God's Just Vengeance: Crime, Violence and the Rhetoric of Salvation*, Cambridge: Cambridge University Press.

Haley, John (1989). "Confessions, Repentance, and Absolution," Martin Wright and Burt Galaway, eds., *Mediation and Criminal Justice: Victims, Community, and Offenders,* Newbury Park, CA: Sage Publications.

McCold, Paul (1997). *Restorative Justice: An Annotated*

Bibliography, Monsey: Criminal Justice Press.

Peachey, Dean (1989). "The Kitchener Experiment", Martin Wright and Burt Galaway, eds., *Mediation and Criminal Justice: Victims, Community, and Offenders,* Newbury Park, CA: Sage Publications.

Pranis, K., Stuart, B., & Wedge. M., (2003.) *Peacemaking Circles – From Crime to Community*. St.Paul, MN: Living Justice Press.

Redekop, Vern (1993). *Scapegoats, the Bible, and Criminal Justice: Interacting with Rene Girard*, Akron PA: Mennonite Central Committee (<http://waynenorthey.com/wp-content/uploads/2016/06/Issue-13.pdf>, last accessed March 19, 2017), last accessed March 19, 2017).

Strong, Karen Heetderks and Dan Van Ness (1997). *Restoring Justice*, Cincinnati: Anderson Publishing Company.

Stuart, Barry (1997). *Community Peacemaking Circles*, Ottawa: Department of Justice.

Tutu, Desmond (2004). *God Has a Dream: a Vision of Hope For Our Time* (New York: Doubleday.

Zehr, Howard (1990). *Changing Lenses: A New Focus for Crime and Justice*, Scottdale: Herald Press.

4

Jesus Is What God Has to Say: A Tabor Meditation

Brian Zahnd

In Appreciation

I remember precisely the first time I heard of Vladika Lazar Puhalo. I was sitting in a coffee shop in downtown Estes Park, Colorado with my friend Brad Jersak as he related an anecdote about the venerable Archbishop. Brad had recently asked Abp. Lazar, "What message would you have for the evangelical church in North America?" Without hesitation Vladika responded, "Your moralism is killing you." As Brad told this story my immediate thought was, "Wow! That Lazar guy nailed it!" *Your moralism is killing you.* It's only five words, but those five words were so prescient regarding the condition of evangelicalism in America that it suggested to me that this Canadian Orthodox theologian had an aptitude for getting to the heart of the matter. A short time later I watched a video Brad Jersak and Ron Dart had recorded with Abp. Lazar on "Deep Structural Fear." In the course of their conversation Vladika said,

> If our faith is primarily a mantra to drive away punishment, our faith isn't really a faith, it is a fear. We feign faith in order to keep from being

punished. When we do that it usually manifests itself as a kind of harsh and brutal moralism. Because in this system it is psychologically comforting to see ourselves as better than other people. Thus trying to hype up our ego leads us to a kind of moralism where we have to denigrate others in order to make ourselves feel better.

I was so impressed with his succinct analysis of how moralism is rooted in fear masquerading as faith that I transcribed it from the video and built a sermon around it. Eventually I came to understand that Abp. Lazar's ability to distil complex subjects into brief, memorable, quotable sentences is a distinctive element of his wisdom. In the conversations I've have had with Vladika over the years—both in Canada and during two of his visits to Missouri—I've always carried away a few gems of this sort.

My first meeting with Abp. Lazar was at his monastery and by sheer coincidence, it happened to be on the occasion of his seventieth birthday. It was also my first substantive conversation with an Orthodox theologian. Among the topics we discussed, I particularly remember conversing about soteriology and hell—big topics for someone raised in the evangelical milieu of America. As it turned out, these are the two aspects of Orthodox theology that I have most fully incorporated into my own thinking, preaching, and writing. I'm not an Orthodox theologian, but my theology of atonement and judgment are thoroughly and unapologetically

Orthodox. My initial meeting with Abp. Lazar no doubt helped establish this trajectory.

After our theological conversation over several cups of tea, Vladika took us to the monastery's print shop where he loaded me down with about thirty books and pamphlets on Orthodox theology, all of which I eventually read and digested. Among the many volumes—most of which were written by Vladika—was a book on icons. It was this book that first awakened in me a deep appreciation for the beauty and theology inherent in iconography—"gospel written in color." Today more than a dozen icons will be found in my home and study—most of them obtained in Jerusalem and Bethlehem. Nearly every morning I have a Christ *Pantokrator* icon and a Crucifixion icon before me when I pray. And all of my books have been written with a Russian cross icon sitting on my desk—I like to think of it as Christ watching over my writing.

As I worked my way through the gift of Orthodox books, Lazar Puhalos's concept of God's eternal disposition toward humankind understood as "co-suffering love" deeply captured my imagination. I'm quite certain that I have used his concept and term—"co-suffering love"—in all of my books. In my earlier books, I attributed the term to Vladika, but today it has become so deeply ingrained in my thinking that I use it quite naturally—but I will always be indebted to Abp. Lazar for this beautiful way of talking about the love of God revealed in Christ.

Along with icons, atonement theology, hell as the

river of God's fiery love, and Vladika's understanding of divine co-suffering love, the other aspect of Orthodox theology that has deeply influenced me is the uniquely Orthodox emphasis on the Transfiguration—or the Uncreated Light of Tabor. Indeed, the Transfiguration is one of the more mysterious stories in the Gospels. Western theology has tended to treat the Transfiguration with scant significance, but the East has seen it as a treasure-trove of theological significance—and here I think the Orthodox instinct is entirely correct. It's from meditating on the Transfiguration that I arrived at this theological axiom: *Jesus is what God has to say.*

The Transfiguration occurred a week after Simon Peter made his great confession about who Jesus is: "You are the Messiah, the Son of the living God" (Matt. 16:16). Jesus responded to Simon's confession by saying, "You are Peter, and on this rock I will build my church" (Matt. 16:18). (This is Jesus's first mention of the church.) A week later Jesus took Peter, James, and John up a high mountain (traditionally believed to be Mount Tabor). Jesus "was transfigured before them, and his clothes became dazzling white, such as no one on earth could bleach them" (Mark 9:2–3). Perhaps the strangest aspect of the Transfiguration is the appearance of Moses and Elijah, who have a conversation with Jesus. The appearance of these two towering figures from the Old Testament contains some obvious and powerful symbolism. Moses the lawgiver and Elijah the prophet are representative figures signifying the Law and the Prophets, or what Christians commonly call the Old

Testament. Peter, James, and John are representative of the church and are witnesses to what happened. On Mount Tabor, Moses and Elijah are summoned from the Old Testament to give their final witness to the anointed Christ who will fulfill what they had begun.

At the beginning of his ministry, Jesus said, "Do not think that I have come to abolish the law or the prophets; I have not come to abolish but to fulfill" (Matt. 5:17). What Moses and Elijah—the Law and the Prophets—had begun, Jesus would fulfill. The goal of the Law and the Prophets was to produce a society of fidelity and justice. Jesus and the kingdom he announces and enacts is where that project finds its fulfillment. The new society formed around Jesus was what the Law and the Prophets were aiming for all along. The Transfiguration is where Moses and Elijah find their great successor. The Transfiguration is where the Old Testament hands the project of redemption and restoration over to Jesus. The Transfiguration is where the old witness (testament) yields to the new witness (testament.)

But initially, Peter misinterpreted what the presence of Moses and Elijah meant. Or to say it in the symbolism of the story, the church misunderstood the relationship of the Old Testament to Jesus. Peter's first impulse was to build three memorial tabernacles on Tabor, treating Moses, Elijah, and Jesus as approximate equals. Peter's implicit suggestion that the Old Testament be given roughly the same authority as Jesus is what we mean when we speak of a "flat reading of the Bible." What can happen with a flat reading of the Bible is that Jesus's teaching of nonviolence in the Sermon on the Mount can be conveniently ignored because we found divine sanction for violence in the Old Testament. In other words, Jesus can be overruled by Moses and Elijah. But Mark tells us how Peter's suggestion for a triumvirate of Moses, Elijah, and Jesus was rebuked on Mount Tabor: "And a cloud overshadowed them, and a voice came out of the cloud, 'This is my beloved Son; listen to him.' And suddenly, looking around, they no longer saw anyone with them *but Jesus only*" (Mark 9:7–8).

Moses and Elijah have left the stage and now only Jesus remains. There's now no possibility of Jesus being upstaged or countermanded by the Old Testament. Jesus is all in all. The Law and the Prophets were the lesser lights in the pre-Christ night sky. They were the moon and stars. They were sent by God, but they were not the fullness of divine light. Israel could grope forward by the moonlight of the Torah; the ancient Hebrews could navigate through the pagan night guided by the constellations of the Prophets. In a world of Stygian darkness, the moonlight and starlight emanating from the Torah and the Prophets made all the difference. But with the coming of Christ, morning has broken, the new day has dawned, and the sun of righteousness has risen with healing in its rays.[1] Now the moon and the stars, Moses and Elijah, the Law and the Prophets are eclipsed by the full glory of God in Christ! The moon and stars recede from view because the sun has risen. When Peter, James, and John looked around on Tabor after the voice from heaven had spoken, they saw only Jesus. This is significant. To say it as plainly as I know how, the Old Testament is not on par with Jesus. The Bible is not a flat text where every passage carries the same weight. This is why Jesus can say things like, "You have heard that it was said, 'An eye for an eye and a tooth for a tooth.' But I say to you, Do not resist an evildoer. But if anyone strikes you on the right cheek, turn the other also" (Matt. 5:38–39).

Where had Jesus's audience heard it said, "An eye for an eye and a tooth for a tooth"? In the Hebrew Scriptures, of course.[2] But Jesus dares to challenge those Scriptures on his own authority. Which is why at the end of his Sermon on the Mount we're told of this reaction from those who heard Jesus: "The crowds were astonished at his teaching. He was teaching them, you see, on his own authority, not like their scribes used to do."[3] Imagine a preacher today saying, "The Bible says, but I say to you…" This is what Jesus is doing. Those listening to Jesus were forced to make a monumental decision: Does Jesus have the authority to challenge the Scriptures? This is why in his book *A Rabbi Talks with Jesus,* Jacob Neusner is uncomfortable with and ultimately rejects the Sermon on the Mount. As he says, "Only God can demand of me what Jesus is asking."[4] Precisely! Rabbi Neusner clearly understands what is at stake. Is Jesus merely an expositor of Scripture, or is he the Word of God in person? The answer to the question is central to what makes a Christian a Christian.

With the "eye for an eye" command, the Old Testament presents a vision of reciprocal justice. Which, in its time, was a vast improvement over unrestrained and ever-escalating retaliatory violence. But Jesus is not a mere echo of Moses. Jesus is taking the revelation of God's nature and God's will far beyond where the Torah ever could. Jesus is not giving the word of God through a Bronze Age cultural filter. Jesus is the Word of God made flesh! This is among the most radical and central claims that Christians make concerning Jesus Christ.

I remember preaching on Jesus's call to the practice of radical forgiveness and being challenged by a church member who said, "Yeah, but the Bible says, 'An eye for an eye, a tooth for a tooth.'" I had to explain to him that a Christian can't cite Moses to silence Jesus. When we try to embrace Biblicism by placing all authority in a flat reading of Scripture and giving the Old Testament equal authority with Christ, God thunders from heaven, "No! This is my beloved Son! Listen to him!"

Though Moses taught that adulterers, rebellious children, and other sinners should be stoned to death, God says to us, "Listen to Jesus!" And Jesus says, "I desire mercy, not sacrifice" (Matt. 9:13). The Pharisees brought a woman to Jesus and said, "Teacher, this woman was caught in the very act of committing adultery. Now in the law, Moses commanded us to stone such women. Now what do you say?" (John 8:4-5). Jesus didn't reply, "Well, you've got a Bible verse. If the Bible says it, I believe it, and that settles it. Where are the rocks? Let's get this stoning started!" No, Jesus says something new: "Let anyone among you who is without sin be the first to throw a stone at her" (John 8:7). That wasn't what the Law said, but Jesus was revealing the heart of God, not giving a conservative reading of the Torah. Jesus gives us a new ethic of life-affirming mercy, which sets aside the old ethic that supported death penalties. Biblicists who desire to condemn sinners to death can quote the Bible by citing Moses. But Jesus says something else. That is why I was so appalled when a well-known evangelical leader wrote an opinion piece for CNN defending the death penalty by citing Moses, yet never once mentioned Jesus.[5] We cannot create Christian ethics while ignoring Christ!

The centrality of Christian ethics is found in Christ himself. Though Elijah called down fire from heaven to burn up his enemies, God says to us, "Listen to Jesus!" And what Jesus says is "Love your enemies" (Matt. 5:44). When a Samaritan village refused hospitality to Jesus and his disciples, James and John wanted to go "shock and awe" on the Samaritans and call down fire from heaven. They did so by finding biblical warrant from the actions of Elijah in the first chapter of 2 Kings. But Jesus didn't say, "Well, that's a biblical principle, all right. So let's nuke 'em!" No, Jesus, says something else: "You do not know what manner of spirit you are of. For the Son of Man did not come to destroy men's lives but to save them" (Luke 9:55–56). War-affirming Biblicists who desire to justify drone strikes and carpet bombing can cite Elijah, but Jesus says something else.

Moses says this. Elijah does that. But Jesus says

and does something completely new and different. And what does God say? Does God instruct us to find a healthy balance between Moses, Elijah, and Jesus? No! God says, "Listen to my Son!" If we want to rummage around in the Old Testament and drag out Moses or Joshua or Elijah or David to mitigate what Jesus teaches about peacemaking and loving our enemies, we are trying to build an Old Testament tabernacle on the holy mountain of Christ's glory, to which God says, "No!"

The role of the Old Testament is to give an inspired telling of how we get to Jesus. But once we get to Jesus we don't build multiple tabernacles and grant an equivalency to Jesus and the Old Testament. This was Peter's mistake on Tabor. Jesus is greater than Moses. Jesus is greater than Elijah. Jesus is greater than the Bible. Jesus is the Savior of all that is to be saved…including the Bible. Jesus saves the Bible from itself! Jesus saves the Bible from being just another violent religious text. Jesus shows us how to read the Bible and not be harmed by it. Jesus delivers the Bible from its addiction to violent retaliation. Moses may stone sinners and Elijah may kill idolaters—and so violent holiness can be justified as biblical—but for a Christian that doesn't matter. We follow Jesus!

It's not biblical principles that we seek to live by but the truth of Christ. Christians don't get to choose in which tabernacle they will be instructed—the tabernacle of Moses, Elijah, or Jesus. The light brighter than the sun shining from the face of Christ on Tabor brings an end to the idea that any other revelation is equivalent to

Christ. The apostle Peter sets forth this high view of Christ when he writes,

> For we did not follow cleverly devised myths when we made known to you the power and coming of our Lord Jesus Christ, but we had been eyewitnesses of his majesty. For he received honor and glory from God the Father when that voice was conveyed to him by the Majestic Glory, saying, "This is my Son, my Beloved, with whom I am well pleased." We ourselves heard this voice come from heaven, while we were with him on the holy mountain. So we have the prophetic message more fully confirmed. You will do well to be attentive to this as to a lamp shining in a dark place, until the day dawns and the morning star rises in your hearts (2 Pet. 1:16–19).

Christian Scripture attests that Jesus is the daybreak of divine revelation who illumines the human heart benighted by primitive darkness. The Bible (in both the Old Testament and the New Testament) does indeed give us the biblical principles for adjudicating the institution of slavery. But that doesn't mean that God endorses slavery. Jesus is what God has to say, and Jesus gives us a trajectory of love that leads us to the abolition of slavery. The Bible may not give a clear repudiation of the institution of slavery, but the living Christ does!

It's not biblical justice that we pursue but Christlike justice. Biblical justice may call for the punitive measures of stoning sinners and executing idolaters, but

Christ clearly calls us to a higher ethic of mercy.

It's not biblical manhood that men should aspire to but Christlike manhood. If we only speak of biblical manhood, who is our pattern? Abraham? Moses? David? Elijah? With their propensity for deceit, anger, adultery, and violence? No, Jesus alone is our model of redeemed manhood.

It's not biblical womanhood that should inform women but the light of Christ. Much of the Bible operates from a cultural assumption that women are the property of their fathers and husbands. But Jesus elevates women to a status of absolute and independent equality.

Wars of conquest, violent retribution, the institution of slavery, and women held as property are all biblical. But when placed in the light of Tabor these primitive assumptions must be renounced. What was once acceptable in the dim light of Moses and Elijah is now rejected in the light brighter than the sun shining from the face of Christ. Today Moses and Elijah (the Law and the Prophets) do one thing: they point to Jesus!

I'm a Christian, not a Biblicist. The Bible is subordinate to Christ. But let me make this clear: I love the Old Testament. I'm a million miles from the second-century heresy of Marcion who regarded the God of the Old Testament as a demiurge and wanted to eliminate the Hebrew Scriptures from the Christian canon. My approach to the Old Testament is nothing like Marcion's. I call the Old Testament sacred Scripture. I read the Old Testament every day. I pray the psalms. I preach the Prophets. I understand the history of Israel as the essential prequel to the story of Christ. But I don't regard the Old Testament as the perfect revelation of God, and I never read the Old Testament without Jesus. Jesus is my sponsor for admission into the Old Testament. (Why else would a Gentile read the ancient Hebrew Scriptures?) I don't read the Law and the Prophets by the light of Moses and Elijah; I read the Law and the Prophets in the light of Christ. So if Moses instructs capital punishment and Elijah models violent retribution, I remember Mount Tabor and the voice from heaven that said, "This is my beloved Son; listen to him" (Mark 9:7). The final testimony of Moses and Elijah is to recede into the background so that Jesus stands alone as the full and true Word of God. Jesus is what God has to say!

The Bible is the written word of God that bears witness to the living Word of God. God did not become a book, but God did become a human being. The Incarnation is not the creation of the canon of Scripture but the virgin birth of Jesus Christ. The Bible is not perfect; parts of it are now obsolete. Surely you admit this. Do you ever worry about violating the biblical prohibition found in Leviticus 19:19: "Nor shall you put on a garment made of two different materials"? Of course not. You understand that part of the Bible to be obsolete as a contemporary command. But nothing about the risen Christ is obsolete. Christ alone is the perfection of God.

The progression of biblical revelation reaches its pinnacle not with Joshua or David but with Jesus Christ.

It's not what Joshua or David said and modeled about violence that is definitive but what Jesus said and modeled about violence. Christian faith is not founded upon violent conquest but upon the crucifixion of a nonviolent Messiah. To set aside what Jesus taught about nonviolence in favor of what we can dig up in the violent conquest narratives of the Old Testament is to turn away from the light of salvation and rush headlong back into the darkness. Amid the contradictory biblical messages on violence, we must always remember that Jesus is what God has to say.

To simply ask what the Bible says about violence yields no simple answer. The Bible gives us a chorus of discordant voices on the subject of violence; it speaks both for and against violence. If the question is whether God is violent or not, and whether violence can be appropriated by God's purposes, both sides can stockpile an arsenal of Bible verses to bolster their positions. But this only leads to a stalemate of conflicting Scriptures. There needs to be some way of adjudicating what texts are definitive in the Bible, especially on the subject of violence. John Dominic Crossan convincingly sets forth how a Christian should decide what is authoritative and what is not.

> The Christian Bible forces us to witness the struggle of these two transcendental visions *within its own pages* and to ask ourselves as Christians how *we* decide between them. My answer is that *we are bound to whichever of these visions was incarnated by and in the his-*

torical Jesus. It is not the violent but the non-violent God who is revealed to Christian faith in Jesus of Nazareth and announced to Christian faith by Paul of Tarsus.

I conclude with an image to hold in imagination.…

As you pass from outer to inner narthex [in Istanbul's Church of St. Savior], the doorway is crowned with a magnificent mosaic of Christ *Pantokrator*.… As in all such Eastern icons, frescoes, or mosaics of Christ, his right hand is raised in an authoritative teaching gesture, with his fingers separated into a twosome and a threesome to command Christian faith in the two natures of Christ and the three persons of the Trinity. As usual, he holds a book in his left hand. But he is not reading the book—it is not even open, but securely closed and tightly clasped.

Christ does not read the Bible, the New Testament, or the Gospel. He is the norm of the Bible, the criterion of the New Testament, the incarnation of the Gospel. That is how we Christians decide between a violent and nonviolent God in the Bible, New Testament, or Gospel. The person, not the book, and the life, not the text, are decisive and constitutive for us.[6]

John Dominic Crossan's simple suggestion is that we allow Jesus to judge all things, including the contradictory passages in the Bible regarding violence. For believers, this approach should not be seen as controversial but deeply Christian. This is not a low view of Scripture but a high view of Christ. Jesus alone is the Alpha and Omega, the full and true Word of God. Jesus is Lord and the final arbiter of all things, even the Bible. *Jesus is what God has to say.*

Endnotes

1. See Malachi 4:2.

2. See Exodus 21:24; Leviticus 24:20; Deuteronomy 19:21.

3. Matthew 7:28–29, as translated by N. T. Wright in *Matthew for Everyone, Part 1: Chapters 1–15* (London: Society for Promoting Christian Knowledge, 2004), 78.

4. Jacob Neusner, *A Rabbi Talks with Jesus* (London: McGill-Queens University Press, 2000), 68.

5. R. Albert Mohler Jr., "Why Christians Should Support the Death Penalty," *Belief* (blog), CNN, May 1, 2014, <http://religion.blogs.cnn.com/2014/05/01/why-christians-should-support-the-death-penalty>.

6. John Dominic Crossan, *God and Empire: Jesus Against Rome, Then and Now* (New York: HarperCollins, 2007), 94–95, italics in the original.

5

Understanding Biblical Violence: An "Oikonomic" Approach

Andrew Klager

Many years, Vladika!
Andrew (Silouan)

When we consider depictions of divine behaviour in the Old and New Testaments, quoting a string of verses to support our favoured portrayal of God typically reveals more about the person who enlists these passages than it does about what the Bible actually says. We can all engage in cafeteria hermeneutics—choosing only those verses that appeal to our theological taste buds—but this is missing the forest for the trees. What's absent, then, is a cohesive interpretive framework for providing at least a bit of consistency.

And yet, neatly packaged solutions to the inconsistency of divine behaviour in the two testaments fail to enter the struggle and remain there if need be. Why, for example, does God seem to authorize genocide (1 Sam. 15), while also preaching peace, love, mercy, and 70x7-fold forgiveness (Matt. 5)? What is the take-away here, and what are we called to imitate and obey? When we ponder Old Testament prescripts through a Christlike lens, is it ever a happy occasion to smash a baby's head against the rocks (Ps. 137:9)? Do any of us stone fortunetellers (Lev. 20:27) or think that God has an evil spirit (1 Sam. 18:10)? Was it that "Satan stood up against Israel, and incited David to count the people of Israel" (1 Chr. 21:1) or was "the anger of the LORD … kindled against Israel, [so that] he incited David against them, saying, 'Go, count the people of Israel and Judah'" (2 Sam. 24:1)? If I'm in a tussle with someone and my wife tries to defend me by grabbing my opponent's nether regions, should I cut off her hand (Dt. 25:11-12)? Or, am I supposed to gradually learn how to love my enemies, pray for those who persecute me, bless those who curse me, forgive my transgressors 70x7-fold, and refuse to fight back—even heal those who are harmed by others who come to my defense—when I face suffering and the prospect of death, all without a weapon in my hands (Mt. 5:43-48)? None of this is meant to discount Scripture or disrespect it, but it does reveal the need for a more consistent hermeneutical framework to make sense of it.

With this in mind, here are a few ingredients to consider. First, when the apostles and Jesus read the Hebrew *Tanakh*, there is little doubt that they revered the prophets who were the mouthpieces of the many "Thus saith the LORD" fiats and dispensations. And yet, the author of Hebrews is fully willing to concede that these prophetic announcements, though helpful at the time they were delivered, were incomplete and could therefore be "topped up" by Jesus—as "the reflection of God's glory and the exact imprint of God's very being" (Heb. 1:3a)—with a more complete revelation of the divine image:

> Long ago God spoke to our ancestors in many and various ways by the prophets, but in these last days he has spoken to us by a Son, whom he appointed heir of all things, through whom he also created the worlds ...[since he is] as much superior to angels as the name he has inherited is more excellent than theirs (Heb. 1:1-2, 4).

So, every jot and tittle of the *Tanakh* was still unfulfilled and therefore incomplete until Jesus arrived as the fullness of God's self-revelation (Mt. 5:18). They lay out the trajectory of the racetrack, but not the finish line.

When the New Testament authors cite these *halakhic* and prophetic words, they serve their own *ad hoc* purpose in light of Jesus' message, example and authority—almost exclusively to show that Jesus is the Messiah—and not for much else, including any sort of self-identification with portrayals of divine wrath that pepper the Old Testament.

One helpful check and balance to authentically draw out the fullness of Scripture is to avoid stringing together a litany of verses that suggest only what the authors and actors *say* and to look also at what they *do*. So, for example, when they quote exclusively from the Septuagint (the Greek translation of the Hebrew *Tanakh* used by the Eastern Orthodox Church), they use a number of different interpretive approaches without any misgivings:

- *Literal*, or quoting passages verbatim;
- *Midrash*, which is a mix of following rabbinical rules for Christian purposes, often conflating oddly paired passages from the Old Testament;
- *Pesher*, which interprets the Old Testament in light of subsequent events, much like a Christocentric and cruciform hermeneutic does;
- *Allegorical*, by which symbolic meaning is extrapolated from the text.

Interestingly enough, a literal reading of the Old Testament is in the minority when we look at all the passages that Jesus and the apostles quote, with Jesus favouring the *pesher* form of interpretations and Paul using *midrashic* methods (likely because of his training as a Pharisee). A few examples:

- Paul quotes Psalm 68 in his epistle to the Ephesians as, "he took many captives and *gave* gifts to his people" (Eph. 4:8), but the original says, "you took many captives; you *received* gifts from people." So, instead of receiving, God does the exact opposite in Paul's paraphrase of this verse.

- Jesus quoted Zechariah 13:7 at the last supper (Mark 14:27), which originally read, "strike down the shepherds and *draw out* the sheep," but he changed it to, "I will strike down the

Shepherd and the sheep will be *scattered*."

- Matthew quotes Zechariah 11:12 (but mistakenly says it's Jeremiah) and isolates the 30 pieces of silver in a simple narrative and transforms it into a prophecy about Judas' betrayal of Jesus, even though this connection isn't in the original text (Matt. 27:9).

These are but a few of the many instances where there is no attempt (or desire) to retain the literal words or meaning of the *Nevi'im* (prophets) or *Ketuvim* (writings), but instead show a willingness to adapt them to specific new situations as they encounter them. These examples may seem minor, but who among us would dare manipulate the text even minimally? Are Jesus and the apostles disrespecting the prophets and Old Testament in general because of their creative and purpose-specific use of Scripture (or, put another way, because they don't treat the Bible as an inerrant celestial textbook as do many conservative Evangelicals)? I don't think they are. Tweaking the words of the *Tanakh* to speak into a specific new and immediate situation—the audience in front of you, in that moment, for a particular purpose or goal—does not undermine their veneration of these prophets. It deepens this reverence.

At issue, however, is the oft-repeated justification of an anthropomorphized, passion-filled, wrathful—even genocidal—deity in the Old Testament who is not only merciful but is also a *just* God. This 'theistic bipolar disorder' allows exponents to imitate this contradictory behaviour (which itself makes God exactly *like* us rather than in any way *better* than us) and lead a generally loving and gentle life while holding out the possibility of meting out retributive justice when circumstances call for it. However, John Howard Yoder (and others) has made the point that those who justify Old Testament violence are actually pleading their case *too much*. This is to say, those who insist on interpreting instances of God's wrath literally or anthropomorphically are un-wittingly providing the means or methods of justifying those actions that none of us actually affirm or follow, including the above examples. So, for example, although we've been desensitized enough by a hyper-militarized society to think violence is sometimes (or even often) fine, what about rape? Do the commandments about and allowances for rape in the Old Testament exhibit God's justice and satisfy his honour? Examples:

1. When 12,000 Israelite soldiers killed the men, women, and children of Jabesh-gilead, there weren't enough women left after the slaughter to satisfy the men of the tribe of Benjamin. So, these were the instructions of the elders:

> "'Go and lie in wait in the vineyards, and watch; when the young women of Shiloh come out to dance in the dances, then come out of the vineyards and each of you carry off a wife for himself from the young women of Shiloh, and go to the land of Benjamin. Then if their fathers or their brothers come to complain to us, we will say to them, 'Be generous and al-low us to *have them*; because we did not cap-

ture in battle a wife for each man. But neither did you incur guilt by giving your daughters to them.' The Benjaminites did so; they *took wives* for each of them from the dancers whom they abducted" (Jdg. 21:20-23a).

2. After an attack on the Midianites,

"Moses became angry with the officers of the army, the commanders of thousands and the commanders of hundreds, who had come from service in the war. Moses said to them, 'Have you allowed all the women to live? These women here, on Balaam's advice, made the Israelites act treacherously against the Lord in the affair of Peor, so that the plague came among the congregation of the Lord. Now therefore, kill every male among the little ones, and kill every woman who has known a man by sleeping with him. But all the young girls who have not known a man by sleeping with him, keep alive for yourselves'" (Num. 31:14-18).

3. There are many other examples such as these, but in terms of rape laws, women were legally bound to marry their rapist (Deut. 22:28-29), and as for rape victims who are married to someone else,

"You shall bring both of them to the gate of that town and stone them to death, the young woman because she did not cry for help in the town and the man because he violated his neighbor's wife" (Deut. 22:24a).

4. Women were also considered "spoils of war" (Jdg. 5:30), and in terms of the celebrated eschatological "Day of the Lord," Zechariah declared,

> "See, a day is coming for the Lord, when the plunder taken from you will be divided in your midst. For I will gather all the nations against Jerusalem to battle, and the city shall be taken and the houses looted and the women raped; half the city shall go into exile, but the rest of the people shall not be cut off from the city" (Zech. 14:1-2). So, apparently rape is also included in the much-anticipated "Day of the Lord."

Do any of us think this is okay? Do any of us truly think this is from God? Is the authorization of rape or punishment of a rape victim an expression of a "just" God? Is this imitable?

Now, given these "deficient," incomplete, often heinous, yet purpose-specific texts, it's important to acknowledge the gradual and incremental self-revelation of God.[1] This unfolding self-revelation re-colours passages that previously fulfilled a particular role, but hundreds of years later are confronted with new circumstances. Thus, they take on new roles or are otherwise corrected and filled-out in line with the commandments of Jesus as "the image of the invisible God" (Col. 1:15). For example, the Old Testament outlines regulations for ritual sacrifice (Lev. 16), but the prophets later say that God doesn't need sacrifices anymore (Isa. 1:11) but instead desires only justice and mercy—which are the same thing, by the way (Mic. 6:6-8)—and Jesus finally comes along as the ultimate sacrifice on the altar of mimetic violence (Lk. 9:23-24) and tells us to imitate it (1 Pet. 2:21). Scripture therefore makes it clear that previous teachings have been reinterpreted in light of new events—particularly the incarnation (Jn. 1:17; Rom. 16:24,25; Heb. 1:1-2).

But what do we do with all of this and how can we find some semblance of consistency? Well, in tandem with what I've already argued,[2] I suggest we embrace the inconsistencies as they appear on the surface but dig deeper underneath to determine what are the more uniform behaviours, beliefs, ideas, encounters, relationships, transfigured lives and contours of a restored cosmos that these various seemingly contradictory words are pointing toward and are trying to direct their specific audiences. What small, incremental movements are they trying to accomplish; what's the trajectory; and what is the goal or *telos*?

To answer this, I'd suggest that the key to understanding inconsistencies in Scripture is acknowledging the *pastoral* function of everything written. In this sense, "pastoral" simply means giving a particular word or instruction in a very specific moment, for a particular person or group, at a specific time, to meet a specific need in order to move the listener(s) gradually toward a greater, more uniform goal or *telos*. The words, then,

Understanding Biblical Violence   77

are a means rather than an end; believing correctly is not the goal, but believing different things that are helpful in different circumstances are vehicles that propel us toward a more meaningful goal—to be "perfect (*teleios* or "mature"), therefore, as your heavenly Father is perfect" (Mt. 5:48). Eastern Orthodoxy, for example, not only emphasizes daily repentance as an expression of this dynamic, but we have the principle of *oikonomia*, where canons are not simply static statements that should be rigidly and uniformly applied in all applicable circumstances, but should instead be *adapted* in a flexible manner to particular situations for the person in front of you in that specific moment.

The principle I would advance then is an "*oikonomic hermeneutic*," where we need to keep our gaze on the *telos* toward which all purpose-specific scriptural passages are pointing. These purpose-specific words include:

- myths that reveal deeper truths about the divine;
- laws given to those who are accustomed to the more familiar Semitic tribal law codes that need to be incrementally tweaked to gradually align with a fuller divine image;
- prophetic pronouncements for their specific audiences, including to the Jews in the Babylonian exile who will eventually return to their homeland;
- warnings against violating God's covenants, and a renewed emphasis on mercy and justice;

- divine and apostolic *kerygma* for specific people who face specific struggles and need to hear specific, unique, tailor-made words for their particular circumstances;
- apocalyptic literature as a form of comfort for those who are suffering persecution at the hand of the most heinous emperor in Rome's history—the "Beast," Nero;
- epistles delivered to several different wayward or otherwise struggling and "green" churches throughout Palestine, Syria, Asia Minor, Greece, and Rome who each needed tailored instructions based on their specific circumstances, issues, and hurdles; and
- apostolic homilies by those who were commissioned to lead the Church after Christ's ascension and the descent of the Holy Spirit.

Each of these larger umbrella categories should, however, be broken down even further into their specific messages to a specific person or group throughout all of Scripture—God's word to Moses is different than Jesus' word to the woman at the well; God's word to Moses at one time is different than his word to Moses at another time; God's instructions to David are different than those that Jesus gives to Nicodemus, or Cornelius, or Zacchaeus.

But why should we read or internalize any of these scriptural passages if they're not specifically directed at us? Well, the importance is not in the literal words themselves (which are only the means, important as they nevertheless are), but in the end or *telos* toward which these seemingly inconsistent words are trying to direct their specific audiences. I.e., what are they all aiming for? What is the goal? What does God want all of us to become? The *telos*, then, is this: God wants to restore his image and likeness in each of us (2 Cor. 3:18; Col. 3:9-10), in cooperation with our partaking of the divine (2 Pet. 1:4), so that we can be compatible enough with the divine to unite with Christ (Jn. 17:20-23).

But in terms of our day-to-day life here on earth, how do we know what Jesus' unfiltered and uniform—and therefore *not* in the purpose-specific tailored pastoral sense—*telos* looks like? I'd suggest that we see it in the only time that Jesus isn't "in control" or deliberately orchestrating (and therefore adapting) his message for a particular audience, but instead *kenotically* submits himself to the coercion and violence of others.

The only time we see his unfiltered and uniform *telos* in action, then, is when Jesus succumbs to death on the cross in self-giving, co-suffering love, mercy, and forgiveness of his enemies. This is the only time that his message (and those of his co-labouring prophets and apostles) is not particular in the pastoral or *oikonomic* sense, but instead purposefully and intentionally universal. Unlike all other instances, it isn't shaped, refined, adapted or tailored for a specific person in a specific circumstance at a specific time, but is the only time that Christ forfeits his own will to endure the coercion of others. This is his unfiltered message of cruciform love, through which he has access to death by his humanity so he can conquer death by his divinity. This, therefore, removes the barrier between humans and the divine to allow us access to the *telos* of transfiguration, of *theosis* that his tailored, varied, seemingly shifting, purpose-specific pastoral or "*oikonomic*" words are meant to point us.

Endnotes

1. Andrew Klager, "Beyond Arguing about Divine Inconsistency in the Old and New Testaments: An Orthodox Perspective on Union and "Knowing," *Clarion Journal* (Feb. 11, 2014).
2. Ibid.

6

We Didn't Fall from Eden— We are Slowly but Surely Crawling Out of Hell

Kevin Miller

With many thanks to Archbishop Lazar Puhalo for his patient instruction, listening ear, and delightful sense of humour, which have served as formidable forces for good in my own intellectual and spiritual development.

"A loathing of modernity is one of the great constants of contemporary social criticism."

So says Steven Pinker in the closing pages of *The Better Angels of Our Nature: Why Violence Has Declined.* Pinker sees such angst underlying many contemporary movements, including environmentalism, religious fundamentalism, aboriginal rights initiatives, and even zombie apocalypse fantasies. Though they look diffcrent on the surface, these trends share one feature in common: a fall from Eden narrative.

Supposedly, in some far-off pre-modern age, we practiced ecological sustainability, family values, religious purity, economic equality, and other seemingly unattainable virtues. But technology destroyed all that. Now we are picking our way through the rubble of the downside of progress with nothing but alienation, ennui, environmental despolation, social pathology, fiscal rapacity, and reality television to keep us warm at night.

Interestingly, even the original Garden of Eden narrative can be interpreted along these lines as a fall from a "pure" hunter-gatherer lifestyle to a rapacious agrarian/urban existence. After eating the forbidden fruit, Adam is expelled from the Garden and cursed to work the land: "Because you listened to your wife and ate fruit from the tree about which I commanded you, 'You must not eat from it,' Cursed is the ground because of you; through painful toil you will eat food from it all the days of your life" (Gen. 3:17).

God goes even further with Cain after Cain murders Abel, saying not even the ground will yield a harvest for him. "Now you are under a curse and driven from the ground, which opened its mouth to receive your brother's blood from your hand. When you work the ground, it will no longer yield its crops for you. You will be a restless wanderer on the earth" (Gen. 4:11–12). So, Cain moves one step further away from a pre-agrarian lifestyle and founds a city, presumably to protect him and his family from his enemies.

The result of this descent from a pure existence in nature to one where humankind is enfolded by technology is a form of violence so ravenous that the only solution in the mind of the Creator is annihilation of virtually the entire human race. But not even that can solve the problem, because the moment humans are let loose on the planet again, they're right back at it with their infernal technology, building the Tower of Babel in an attempt to unseat their Creator.

Concluding that "flooding an ideology out of existence" is futile, that even divine violence merely begets new and more complicated forms of violence, God attempts a different strategy with Abram, calling him away from human sacrifice and human civilization period. If Abram and his people are to encounter God, that can only happen in the wilderness. It's a return to Eden, if you will, which culminates with the wandering Israelites' arrival in Canaan, a land flowing with milk and honey. However, the land has been seized by those nefarious users of technology—the Hittites, the Amorites, the Canaanites, the Perizzites, the Hivites, and the Jebusites. If the Israelites are to truly regain Eden, these techno-criminals must go.

I could go on with this interpretation, showing how the same anti-technology narrative might underlie the storming of Jericho, for example, which was done without weapons or any other form or technology, or God's warnings about not adopting a monarchial form of government, which would make the people subject not only to the king but also his machines of war. But that may be stretching things a little. My point is, if such an interpretation of even the original Fall narrative is at all correct, it would suggest that our pessimism about technology is nothing new. Perhaps a permanent aspect of the human psyche is a Janus-like tendency to walk backwards into the future, forever viewing the past through rose-coloured glasses, because the reality of the future is simply too terrible to bear. Why is the future so terrible? Because that is where we will have to deal with the consequences of the mistakes we make in the present.

While I sympathize and often fall victim to this view, I see the fall from Eden narrative as one of the most prevalent and destructive myths afflicting our culture. The minute we fall for it, the hunt for scapegoats begins. Who is responsible for our fall from grace? In previous generations, we tended to target witches, heretics, the Jews, or even Satan, believing they had somehow infected our culture with their evil. If only these enemies could be eliminated, we could return to our original state of grace. The problem is, this so-called solution has never worked. Only in retrospect do we realize the futility of our efforts and the grievous consequences of our actions. And yet, we repeat them over and over again once a new enemy has been identified.

These days, our finger of accusation has shifted away from the perennial scapegoats of history to anything that's big—Big Government, Big Pharma, Big Agriculture, Big Oil. In other words, the primary users (and abusers) of technology. They are the despoilers of the planet, or so we believe. If only we could find some way to stamp them out, we could finally experience that utopia for which we all yearn.

I see two forces at work beneath the fall from Eden narrative, particularly concerning our ambivalence toward technology. The first is our short cultural memory. If you read Pinker's book or Jared Diamond's *Guns, Germs and Steel,* for instance, you will quickly realize that romantic ideas of better days gone by are nothing but a cruel illusion. The history of humanity prior to innovations like modern medicine, electricity, fossil fuel-powered transportation, pesticides, fertilizers, and so on is a history of war, famine, disease, misery, suffering, and death. I'm talking about 99.9 percent of human history here. Maybe more. As Pinker puts it,

> our ancestors were infested with lice and parasites and lived above cellars heaped with their own feces. Food was bland and monotonous, and intermittent. Health care consisted of the doctor's saw and the dentist's pliers. Both sexes [and children] laboured from sunrise to sundown, whereupon they were plunged into darkness. Winter meant months of hunger, boredom, and gnawing loneliness in snow-bound farmhouses.
>
> But it was not just mundane physical comforts that our recent ancestors did without. It was also the higher and nobler things in life, such as knowledge, beauty, and human connection.
>
> Here is where unsentimental history and statistical literacy can change our view of modernity. For they show that nostalgia for a peaceable past is the biggest delusion of all. We know that native peoples, whose lives are romanticized in today's children's books, had rates of death from warfare that were greater than those of our world wars. The romantic

visions of medieval Europe omit the exquisitely crafted instruments of torture and are innocent of the thirtyfold greater risk of murder in those times.

The moral commonplaces of our age, such as that slavery, war, and torture are wrong, would have been seen as saccharine sentimentality, and our notion of universal human rights almost incoherent. Genocide and war crimes were absent from the historical record only because no one at the time thought they were a big deal.[1]

We may have invented the term "genocide" in the twentieth century (and more efficient means by which to carry it out), but the genocides we committed (are committing) are far from historical aberrations. They are merely business as usual under a new name. And the fact is, we are committing fewer of them than ever before.

The second factor that gives life to the fall from Eden narrative is our tendency to locate evil "out there" rather than within ourselves. We do this, because it is the path of least resistance. Defeating evil out there is far easier than confronting our own heart of darkness, which requires courage, humility, and self-sacrifice. When faced with such a high calling, it's so much easier to point the finger and pull the trigger. No need to think, no need to feel, and no need to fear. We think we can defeat evil the same way we defeat zombies, with a bullet to the brain—a cinematic metaphor for the futility of trying to bomb an ideology out of existence. No matter how many zombies we kill, they just keep coming. And when we have to confront living, breathing humans who are not part of our little group, that's when everything really breaks down.

Such apocalyptic fantasies aside, to quote Ben J. Wattenberg, "The good news is the bad news is wrong."[2] Contrary to some of our deepest-held convictions, we didn't fall from Eden. Instead, we have slowly but inexorably been crawling out of the hell of history. Much of the world is still mired deep within that hell, and there's no guarantee we won't all plunge back into it again (another fear manifested by zombie apocalypse fantasies), but I don't think it will be technology that takes us there. Rather, it will be our own pessimism, even as people claim their quest for Eden is bringing us closer to heaven. In truth, technology is our only ticket out of this hell, because technology is nothing but a manifestation of human ingenuity in the face of difficulty, although history and countless science fiction stories stand as a warning that even technology created with the best of intentions can sometimes turn against us.

As science writer Ronald Bailey says, Wagering against human ingenuity has always been a bad bet." Unfortunately, anyone mired in the fall from Eden myth is placing this bet every day. They think they're putting their money on black, but no matter how many times we spin the wheel, it's guaranteed to keep coming up red.

One might argue that the "myth of progress" can be just as destructive and can easily lead to a hunt for scapegoats—who is inhibiting our forward momentum? Eliminate them! I don't deny this possibility. However, I can't help but think that, in the long run, an optimistic approach to life that encourages ingenuity and innovation and presumes the best of others will lead not only to a reduction in scapegoating but will also take us further than an approach that constantly tries to rein people in for fear of what they might do if they take hold of the unbridled potential with which we have been bestowed.

Endnotes

1. Steven Pinker, *The Better Angels of Our Nature: Why Violence Has Declined* (Viking Books, 2011), 293.
2. Ben J. Wattenberg, *The Good News is the Bad News is Wrong* (Simon & Schuster/Touchstone, 1984).

7

Sailing into the Winter Sun

Archbishop Lazar Puhalo

Above all, remember the love, hope and peace we have in Jesus Christ. Never doubt the love of God.
—Abp. Lazar Puhalo

Learn the meaning of life: to love and be loved. Nothing is more important than forgiveness.

Faith and forgiveness are the surest imitation of Christ, but we need to pray for grace to have enough love in order to forgive.

The whole gospel is summarized in the parable of the Prodigal Son. If people could only understand that the parable is first of all about God.

Everything is forgiven. Everything.

If Christ can say, "Father forgive them" even from the Cross, we have no excuse for not forgiving people.

God doesn't punish. God never harms his people. The trouble is that he respects us and our choices. That is where 'punishment' comes in.

It is difficult because sometimes the Fathers speak about punishment and at other times, about forgiveness. But ultimate punishment is the radiance and glory of the love of Christ IF somehow it were possible you had to spend eternity without it.

"Vengeance is mine." Not that God takes vengeance. Rather, that you aren't worthy of revenge and God is saying, "I am withholding it from you."

Some hearts are attracted to the most violent parts in Scripture, like a magnet to their own hearts. What's inside them attracts them to those texts. For each speaks out of the fullness of his own heart, and so they should, since we can't really fake it. But God doesn't take vengeance. He simply withholds it from us. We wouldn't know what to do with it anyway.

The Psalmist says, "Thy mercy will pursue me," not merely 'follow me,' because Mercy forever wants to catch you.

The wicked conscience is the fire that never dies. People pass their own sentence by the way they judge. But there is such thing as the wicked conscience: if you think God is evil—you make him to be evil. Then we create a god in the image of our own hearts. Then God is not just a giant person, but a giant ME.

Some act as if God were waiting for the end of the world to punish everyone, by which they mean, everyone who disagrees with me.

No, God is love. Know God is love.

It is not possible to love and want vengeance.

God has for us nothing but grace, mercy and love. Never doubt the love of God.

The Cross: The Cross is not only a trophy of victory, but a trophy of co-suffering love that surpasses the universe—the love that holds back nothing and gives life. Seeing the sign of the victory of co-suffering love gives us strength and hope to carry on.

Instructions for the Clergy

We need to be compassionate because sin is an illness.

Confession: The priest's job is to help people forgive themselves so they don't become sick with guilt—to ask God's forgiveness and know that they have it. We are commanded not to judge another man's servant but we are the servants of the Lord, so we should be careful how we judge ourselves. So, don't be so hard on yourself that your guilt makes you sick.

Shame is the degradation of another human being. The priest should never do that. Shaming another person is an act of malice. It is not effective or useful.

In confession, the priest says "I, an unworthy sinner, have no power on earth to forgive sin but God alone has this power." The priest must never think that it is he who is forgiving sin. God is forgiving sin through the Church." I am only an agent, called to communicate God's forgiveness.

We must not create artificial rules and impose regulations to prepare for communion. Our preparation is to forgive one another and remove any malice from our hearts. Stalin himself could read three canons but that would not prepare him for communion.

We are to be priests, not policemen. Confession is not about investigating others' sin, but about readying them to receive the Eucharist. Encourage people to receive communion rather than hindering them. People know in their own hearts if there is an impediment and abstain from communion. Remember, according to Ignatius the God-bearer, we are administering the medicine of immortality. Communion is not a reward for virtue. It is a medicine for the weak and the fallen. Even in the canons of Alexandria, when Timothy of Alexandria was asked if people possessed by demons could receive communion, he replied, "Yes, but not as often as others—only once a week."

The Liturgy: We serve according to the Fathers. Read the Fathers and assimilate the Liturgy as heart knowledge and not just choreography. We use the basic Greek Typikon, so go straight from Great Doxology into the Divine Liturgy.

When we begin the Liturgy, we open the Holy Doors because the gates of Paradise have been reopened. As the Troparian says, "Christ is risen. The gates of Paradise are open, never to be closed again." So the Holy Doors should never be closed during the Liturgy except perhaps for the Priests' communion. The habit of closing the Holy Doors during the Liturgy is meaningless. It depends only what kind of jewelry the priest gets to wear and has nothing to do with the meaning of the Liturgy. *Do not shut what Christ has opened.*

The priest begins the Liturgy by raising the Gospel in the air and making the sign of the Cross with it—the *Cross is the key that unlocks the gates of paradise.*

The priest should *cense* the people with at least as much attention and reverence as the icons, since the people are the living icons of God.

Preaching: The sermon is an integral part of the Liturgy. Some priests use it as an opportunity to scold or nag people instead of giving them an uplifting message taken from the Gospel or epistle reading for the day. We are children of the promise, not the law, so our *sermons need to reflect above all the love, hope and peace we have in Jesus Christ.*

Consecration of the Holy Gifts: The priest should go out through the Holy Gates to say, "Let us lift up our hearts, and let us give thanks unto the Lord. According to St. John Chrysostom, the priest does not return to the Holy Place and continue until he hears the assent of the people, "It is meet and right so to do." The hymn that follows "It is meet and right" is an addition that doesn't belong. And in any case, it should be kept quite distinct from the people's assent, "It is meet and right."

Remember that the people are a Royal Priesthood, a special people, according to the Apostle Peter.

When the gifts are consecrated, the people should exclaim the "Amens."

Remember that the altar is a type of Paradise. And the chalice becomes the tree of life that grew in the midst of Paradise. Liturgy is all about preparing and drawing the people to partake the banquet. The Liturgy is eschatological in that we are at the wedding feast of heavenly Groom and His earthly bride.

The Agape meal after the Liturgy is part of worship and a continuation of worship because that is where we fellowship and at least try to love one another.

The great moral imperative of Jesus Christ is the New Commandment that we *love one another as Christ loved us.*

Authors

Archbishop Lazar Puhalo

Archbishop (ret.) Lazar Puhalo is the founding Abbot of All Saints Orthodox Monastery, first established in Rosedale, BC in 1969, now in Dewdney, BC since 1991.

Ron S. Dart

Ron Dart teaches in the Department of Political Science/ Philosophy/Religious Studies at University of the Fraser Valley, where he has served since 1990.

Brad Jersak

Brad Jersak is a preacher and reader at All Saints of NA Monastery. He serves on faculty at St. Stephen's University (NB) and is editor-in-chief of *CWR magazine*.

Wayne Northey

Wayne Northey was BC Director of M2/W2 (Man-to-Man/Woman-to-Woman Restorative Christian Ministries) 1998 to 2014. He has been a leading advocate of restorative justice in Canada since 1974.

Brian Zahnd

Brian Zahnd is the founder and lead pastor of Word of Life Church in St. Joseph, Missouri, where he has served for over 30 years.

Andrew Klager

Andrew is the founder and director of *IRPJ* (the Institute for Religion, Peace and Justice, St. Stephen's University) and serves other academies on faculty and administration.

Kevin Miller

Kevin Miller is an author, editor, filmmaker and educator. He was the producer, writer and director of the documentary movie *Hellbound?* which featured Abp. Lazar.

Clarion
Journal of Spirituality & Justice
Vol. 1, 2003 contents

Editors:

Brad Jersak, Ron Dart, Kevin Miller, Derek Weiss

Art:

Jordan Neufeld, Sara Borck, Angela Funk

Articles:

Brad Jersak, "Where faith and justice meet" (editorial)

Ron Dart, "Justice and spirituality: the vision of the Beatitudes" (editorial)

Ryan Santschi, Poem (untitled)

Gay-Lynn Voth, "Empty"

Eric H. Janzen, "Heart-cry of the Father"

Andrew MacPherson, "The way to his image"

Michelle Wiebe, "Love"

Stephen Klaue, "Meeting 'the man'"

Michelle Wiebe, "I see Jesus"

Wayne Northey, "The mother of all heresies"

Chris Janzen, "Sleeping bombs" (poem)

Derek Weiss, "Residual guilt"

Nathan Rieger, "Hidden beauty, hidden brokenness"

Lane Walker, "Just neighbors"

Brad Jersak, "The bride" (poem)

Bill Pegg, "Cries" and "Stop" (poems)

Karen Dart, "Coal Diamond" (haiku)

Jordan Neufeld, "Worship"

Desiree Myers, "Union"

Ron Dart, "Crosshairs"

CPSIA information can be obtained
at www.ICGtesting.com
Printed in the USA
LVHW081602130519
617630LV00042B/1633/P